The Way of Paradox

The Way of Paradox

Spiritual Life as taught by Meister Eckhart

CYPRIAN SMITH OSB

Paulist Press
New York, N.Y.   Mahwah, N.J.

This book was first published in 1987 by
Darton, Longman and Todd Ltd
89 Lillie Road, London SW6 1UD

© 1987 Cyprian Smith osb

ISBN: 0–8091–2948–5

First published in the United States by
Paulist Press, 997 Macarthur Blvd.,
Mahwah, N.J. 07430

Printed and bound in Great Britain

Contents

Contents

Acknowledgements

We are grateful to Element Books Ltd for permission to quote from M. O'C. Walshe's *Meister Eckhart: Sermons and Treatises* and to Octagon Books for permission to quote from *Treatises and Sermons of Meister Eckhart* edited by James M. Clark and John V. Skinner.

Introduction

This is not a scholarly book, though scholarship has gone into it. It aims rather at helping the modern spiritual seeker, by putting him in touch with the mind of Meister Eckhart, one of the greatest spiritual teachers of all time.

Since many of Eckhart's own works are now available in excellent English translations, one might ask whether it would not be better to go to them directly, without bothering about this book. But Eckhart, though a very fascinating and magnetic author, is not by any means always easy to understand, without some preliminary explanation and introduction. It is not that his style is verbose or obscure, far from it. But he deals with deep matters, which strain our powers of linguistic expression to the utmost; and he often talks, too, in the language of metaphor and daring paradox, in order to convey his overwhelming vision of God. This has led some to misunderstand him seriously, and read their own ideas into him. There have been lamentable cases of this during the last hundred years. Therefore I am trying, in this book, to give a clear and balanced account of his teaching in the belief that it is deep, life-giving and of great value in the modern world.

Since this spiritual teaching is so rich, many-sided and paradoxical, a word of advice is perhaps needed to all those who read this book. If any readers start it and find they dislike it, then let them put it away and forget about it. But if they do like it and want to go on, then they should read it slowly, carefully and, above all, read it right through to the end. Only in that way can they see it in proper perspective and understand how it all fits together.

A final word on the overall structure of the book. The first two chapters are introductory, dealing with the interest and value of this spiritual teaching of Eckhart's in the contem-

porary world, and of his vision of the spiritual life as a tension
of opposites. The central chapters deal with the various
elements in this tension, culminating in the figure of Christ,
in whom the tension teaches its maximum point and achieves
its reconciliation, both in history and in the human heart.
The final chapters deal with special problems of everyday
living, and the implications of Eckhart's teaching for the
spirituality of today and tomorrow.

CYPRIAN SMITH

1 *Light in the Darkness*

The aim of this book is very simple. It is to try to express, clearly and intelligibly, the main elements in Eckhart's teaching on the spiritual life, so that modern people may be able to grasp them and use them. Is there a real need for this? I think so. Though Eckhart was condemned in his own lifetime, and almost completely forgotten in the centuries that followed, he never disappeared totally from sight, and during the last hundred years there has been a steadily increasing interest in him, culminating in our own time, when he is at last fully emerging into the light again. His writings have a fascination and attractiveness uniquely their own, which not only draw a great number of people but also a wide variety of very different people. Protestants and Catholics, believers and unbelievers, Buddhists and Hindus, not to mention that great expert on the human mind, the psychologist C. G. Jung – all these have felt the magnetism of Eckhart and responded to it, each in his own way. There is something about him which appeals to modern people; there is some widely felt need which he seems able to answer. What is it?

We live today in an age of transition, in which traditional ways of thinking and living are passing away, yet new ways have not yet been found to replace them. This generates doubt and confusion and, above all, a sense of profound dissatisfaction. Is it not this, rather than sheer malice and destructiveness, which underlies much contemporary violence – the often sporadic and pointless violence of the terrorists, for example, or of young people in city streets? When a society and culture has grown old, and is felt to have outlived its value, that automatically generates restlessness and a desire for radical change, even, if necessary, by violent and ruthless means . . . It does not take a prophet or a visionary

to recognize that Apocalypse is in the air, the conviction that
society and culture as we know it is drawing to an end, that
its time is running out. This theme is constantly cropping up
today, in films, in painting and poetry, and in novels
especially – a whole host of science-fiction novels are built
upon it, as well as more serious and reflective work such as
C. S. Lewis's *That Hideous Strength*. And anyone who has
worked in church circles cannot fail to observe how people
immediately sit up and take notice when the threatening
prophecies are read out from the Book of Revelation, but
seem to be in no way reassured by the vision of the heavenly
Jerusalem which follows! Why should this be, since both
prophecies belong to Scripture, and are therefore presumably
both inspired? But in a world threatened with injustice, violence and the possibility of nuclear holocaust, it is the pessi-
mistic prophecy which strikes home, because it is closer to
experience . . . and also, perhaps, to desire.

This dissatisfaction, restlessness and desire for radical
change extends into the spiritual sphere as well. This is bound
to be so. Religion is concerned with the deepest aspirations
of the human race; it touches the deepest levels of the human
heart. But in doing this it evolves particular methods of
teaching, worshipping, guiding and helping which bear the
imprint of a particular society and culture. There can come
a time when these methods, these outward forms, no longer
answer the deepest needs of humanity. There develops a rift
between what people, however obscurely, feel they need, and
what the existing religions are actually able to give them.
Thus in the heart of the Church itself, and also in the heart
of the non-Christian religious communities, there develops
the Apocalyptic syndrome, the longing for radical change at
all costs.

It is this, surely, which is the main reason behind our half-
empty churches, and the general decline of religious interest,
especially among the young. This lack of interest in traditional
religion is no doubt partly due to carelessness and inertia, to
the shoddy values of a materialistic society which expects
quick returns with the minimum of effort. But there is surely
more to it than that. Anyone who has worked or lived for any
length of time with young people will have found them much
interested in spiritual matters. The desire, the aspiration, is

very definitely there, but traditional, organized and insti-
tutional religion is not managing to channel it or direct it.
Therefore it flows into channels of its own choosing – Eastern
religions, transcendental meditation, or into dangerous and
destructive substitutes for religion, such as magic and
occultism, drugs, violence and sex. The spiritual impulse is
alive but no longer corresponds to the outward religious
forms. The Catholic Church recognized the existence of this
crisis, and sought to tackle it, in the Second Vatican Council.
Much was achieved then, and much is still being achieved.
But it needs to go further, and we have to ask ourselves: what
are the most urgent spiritual needs of the present time, and
how are they to be met?

Amid the general unrest and disquiet among religious
people today, two main desires can be seen coming to the
surface. They have been observed and commented on already
by a number of people, but it is well worth drawing attention
to them again, for they are fundamental. The first is political
and social. It is the desire for freedom, for a more just and
equitable society. The second is more inward and personal.
It is the desire to learn about the human heart, its inner
depths and recesses. Within the Church, it manifests itself as
a desire to learn more about prayer and meditation, about
different levels of consciousness and awareness. These two
desires, social and mystical, are interconnected and cannot
be divorced from one another. They must be explored simul-
taneously, because the one inevitably affects the other. There
is much about ourselves and our own hidden depths which
can only be discovered by living with others, by experiencing
the contact – sometimes the clash – with personalities very
different from our own. So the communal element, the social
and political dimension, cannot be ignored. But it is equally
true that we cannot hope to understand or change society
unless we also learn to understand and change ourselves. We
have to know, recognize and accept what is going on in
the deepest levels of our mind, for this affects our outward
behaviour. There is nothing in politics or society which has
not originated in the human mind. Whatever the human
heart, in its secret depths, conceives and imagines, for good
or ill, will manifest itself outwardly in time. The scientific,
technologized world we live in today was born in the minds

of French philosophers of the Enlightenment before taking shape in concrete reality. Also, the unconscious desires and aspirations which we have are sometimes the very opposite of what we are consciously trying to achieve. We may think we are working for peace, justice and the good of others, when in fact we are seeking power, domination and the subjection of others to our own selfish ends. Apparently good and altruistic actions are often vitiated by unconscious motives. The modern psychologists have shown us that. Great spiritual teachers, both Christian and non-Christian, have gone a step further and taught down the ages that actions which are good in themselves, if done for unworthy motives, however unconscious, will turn in the end to harm. Therefore we need to explore our inner depths; we need to know ourselves.

It is in this field that Eckhart comes into his own. He was born in the thirteenth century, when the Christian Church, with all its doctrines, liturgies, sacraments and power-structures, was very highly developed. As a Dominican friar, thoroughly trained in theology and philosophy, and entrusted by his Order with important teaching and administrative posts, he knew the Church, and its outward forms, inside out. But at the same time he had a profound knowledge of the human heart, and a burning desire to find out *what* it is in human beings that makes them desire God and able to be united with him. In this area he made important discoveries, which rank him with the greatest spiritual teachers of all time. He realized, above all, that the question of God is at the same time a question about Man. I cannot know God unless I know myself. Religion has its origin and its meaning in the human heart. Therefore, when the outward forms cease to satisfy, it is only by returning to the human heart that we can resolve the crisis. The sublime and glorious reality which we call 'God', is to be sought first and foremost in the human heart. If we do not find him there, we shall not find him anywhere else. If we do find him there, we can never lose him again; wherever we turn, we shall see his face.

This is perhaps the secret of Eckhart's appeal for modern people; the fact that he knows what human beings are like, what their truest and deepest needs are. This sort of knowledge is precious, and even priceless, for it alone makes it possible to really help people. Mere goodwill is not enough:

in order to help people we have to know what their real needs are; we have to know *them*. That is why so many people today turn to the psychologist and the psychiatrist, rather than to the priest or the minister; it is not necessarily that they will get *answers* from the psychologist, but they feel nevertheless that they will be truly known and understood by him, and that is already a great deal. It is a large part, perhaps almost all, of what they want.

This knowledge and understanding of what human beings really are, what lies in the deeper levels of the human heart, ought to be found in the Church, for it is religion, above all, which seeks to touch the central core of human nature. But people who turn to priests and spiritual directors for this kind of help are often disappointed. The Church claims, like Jesus himself, to know 'what is in man' (Jn 2:25). But does it? Jung points out, very pertinently, that in the eyes of official religion the human psyche, with all its hidden folds and dark declivities, has no real existence of its own; for the priest the psyche or soul is just something to be fitted into a dogmatic and liturgical framework. This does not satisfy the modern seeker, who wants above all to be understood for what he is, to be brought to the realization and acceptance of what really does lie in the innermost depths of his mind, regardless of whether this fits in with official church dogma or not. He feels, with some justification, that there must be something wrong with dogma which is not related to human facts as they are experienced. It is no use my being told that I am 'redeemed' by Christ, if my actual experience is one of alienation, darkness and self-division, even when in the heart of the Church, the community of believers. That is why so many turn to the psychiatrist rather than the priest. It is also why so many turn to Buddhist, Hindu and Sufi teachers; they believe – often rightly – that they will find in them a profound and detailed science of the inner life of the mind, a sureness of touch in practical guidance and training, which is rarely equalled within the Christian fold.

But before we turn East for the guidance and knowledge which we need, would it not make sense to look first at our own Christian tradition, in case what we are looking for is already there, under our noses, though we do not see it? If we do this, Eckhart will be one of those who can give us most help, for although he is no longer alive, to speak to us directly, his works live on and touch closely on the matters which concern us. He understands very clearly that spiritual life only has meaning when it is related to what goes on inside us. It is no use preaching Christ to people so long as Christ is seen merely as someone external to ourselves, a vague, shadowy figure who spoke a foreign language and died 2000 years ago. We need to be led to know and experience Christ as a living force within us, energizing, healing, making and unmaking, leading us to greater awareness, compassion and wholeness. So Eckhart writes:

> St Augustine says: 'What does it avail me that this birth (the birth of Christ, the Son of God, in eternity) is always happening, if it does not happen in me? That it should happen in me is what matters.' We shall therefore speak of this birth, of how it may take place in us and be consummated in the virtuous soul.[1]

For him, as we shall see, God is above all a reality to be experienced from within, and this is a truth which speaks profoundly to the modern age and, indeed, to any age of transition and crisis.

But we trust most the teacher who himself embodies the doctrine he teaches, who has himself trod the path he points out to others. If Eckhart really has this knowledge, where did he get it from? What experiences did he pass through, what inner conflicts, setbacks and triumphs? Here we enter the domain of mystery. Tantalizingly little is known of Eckhart's life, what sort of character he had, what experiences shaped and moulded him. The little we do know can be summed up in few words, which may give us some clue to what we are trying to find out.

He was born around 1260 in Hochheim, a village near the town of Erfurt in Thuringia – now in East Germany. Around 1275 he entered the Dominican priory at Erfurt, and the cool, spacious church where he worshipped with his fellow-Dominicans, still stands, though the other buildings of the priory have gone. He soon showed himself an intelligent pupil, and was sent for his theological training to the Studium Generale in Cologne. Albert the Great, one of the greatest minds of the age, was still alive in Cologne at that time,

1. Walshe, vol. 1, p. 1.

though very old, and it is likely that Eckhart met him. He
may even have been taught by him; a number of respectful
and affectionate references to Albert in several sermons
suggest this. Until 1325 his life was divided into periods spent
in Paris – where he became renowned for his skill as scholar,
lecturer and disputator – and periods spent in Germany,
where his Order appointed him to important administrative
posts, thus showing that his skills were by no means exclusively intellectual or spiritual. In 1302 he received his degree
from the University of Paris; and thereafter came to be known
as 'Meister' or 'Master'. It is curious that this standard
academic title should have stuck to him right down to the
present day, so that he is the only medieval theologian still
referred to by it. Yet perhaps it is appropriate – especially if
we regard him as a 'Master' in a sense deeper than the merely
academic.

In 1323 he returned to the Studium Generale in Cologne.
By this time he had become famous, greatly admired for the
holiness of his life and for his many gifts as administrator,
scholar, preacher and spiritual director. It therefore came as
an enormous shock when the Archbishop of Cologne, Hein-
rich von Virneburg, instigated proceedings against him for
heresy. The virulence and determination of the Archbishop's
hostility has led many to wonder what caused it. Part of it
was no doubt due to the often acrimonious rivalry between
Dominicans and Franciscans at that time – the Archbishop
himself was a Franciscan. There was also a great proliferation
of heresies in Cologne, especially among laypeople, among
whom Eckhart seems to have had a considerable following,
and the Archbishop was determined to get this situation
under control, often using extremely harsh measures in order
to do so. But Eckhart also laid himself open to danger by the
boldness of his language, the novelty of his ideas and the
baffling, often paradoxical way he expressed those ideas. All
this contributed to his downfall. In retrospect, bearing in
mind the increasingly repressive attitude of the Church authorities, there seems nothing surprising about this. What is
surprising is not that Eckhart was finally tried for heresy but
that he had got away with so much for so long.

Two clerics compiled a list of statements which they alleged
Eckhart to have made at different times, and which they

claimed were heretical. He conducted his own defence, and it would be pleasant if we could say that he did so ably. At times, however, it seems that he did not. He was already an old man, and his powers were doubtless on the wane, though much of what he said in reaction to his accusers was penetrating and very much to the point. In 1327, he made a solemn declaration in the cathedral of Cologne that he had no intent to teach or preach heresy. The Vicar-General and Visitor of the German Dominican Province, Nicholas von Strasbourg, intervened in his defence, but was overruled by the Archbishop. The proceedings had by now been dragging on for a long time, so Eckhart appealed to the Pope. The Archbishop, still determined to get his man, quashed the appeal, but he was too late. The appeal had already reached Rome, and the authorities had begun to act. It was decreed that a second trial would be held, at Avignon, where Eckhart accordingly went, intending to defend himself as he had in Cologne. This trial was a much more serious and carefully conducted affair than the previous one. The principal judge was a learned theologian, Cardinal Jacques Fournier – later to be Pope Benedict XII – a fair-minded man who seems to have been anxious to do justice to Eckhart. Nevertheless, the legal machinery for assessment and judgement was cumbersome and archaic, centred as it was on a selection of statements or propositions from the accused man's work, quoted without regard to their context. It was not a process greatly conducive to the proper understanding of a man's thought, and the Cardinal himself protested at its insufficiency. The Pope then reigning, John XXII, had further appointed a commission to draw up a fresh list of allegedly heretical statements by Eckhart. While these were being examined, Eckhart died, sometime before 30 April 1328. Thus he did not live to see the Pope promulgate the Bull *In Agro Dominico*, in which twenty-six of his statements were listed, fifteen of them declared heretical and eleven 'ill-sounding and suspect'. The condemnation did not refer to Eckhart personally – he was said to have deplored and revoked his errors – but only to the listed statements and the books containing them. Eckhart had always shown complete obedience and loyalty to the Pope, and perhaps it was in recognition of this that the Pope waited for Eckhart to die before issuing the condemnation.

Ironically, John XXII was later to be condemned himself by his successor, Jacques Fournier, for a heresy concerning the Beatific Vision and the Last Judgement.

The whole situation has been very aptly summed up by Peter Hebblethwaite: 'Thus we have a heretical Pope who denounces as a heretic Eckhart, whose work he had not read and whose defence he had not heard.'[2]

What does this tell us about Eckhart the man, and about the way in which he acquired his knowledge and experience of the spiritual life? Not a great deal, but there are at least two points we should note on the basis of what we know.

First, his life was extremely busy and active. From some of what he says in his sermons, we might be tempted to picture him as a hermit and ascetic, lost in solitary contemplation. That cannot be right. His Order elected him to be Prior of Erfurt, then first Provincial of Saxony, and in 1307 Vicar-General of Bohemia. These were important and responsible posts, involving administrational skill, teaching, and much travelling (on foot). If we suppose, then, that he was given to ecstatic meditation in solitude, it is hard to see when he could have done it. He clearly had some skill as an administrator, so he was not at all the kind of starry-eyed mystic whose raptures are bought at the price of chronic ineptitude in practical affairs. A great part of his teaching is on the question of what we might call 'contemplation in a world of action', how to maintain the unified and tranquil vision of God while immersed in the everyday world of bustle and activity. This is a problem very real to the twentieth century, and we may safely assume that what Eckhart has to say about it is based on his own experience.

Second, he knew, as we do, what it is like to live in a declining culture on the threshold of profound change and revolution. Fourteenth-century Europe was anything but a settled and tranquil place. Though the traditional structures of power, spiritual and temporal, were still there, and adorned with much outward magnificence, there was much unrest, violence, injustice and insecurity. Then, as today, the yearning for Apocalypse was present.

The feeling of general insecurity which was caused by the chronic

2. *The Tablet*, 9 August 1986, p. 832.

form wars were apt to take, by the constant menace of the
dangerous classes, by the mistrust of justice, was further aggra-
vated by the obsession of the coming end of the world, and by
the fear of hell, sorcerers and devils. The background of all life
in the world seems black. Everywhere the flames of hatred arise
and injustice reigns. Satan covers a gloomy earth with his sombre
wings. In vain the militant Church battles, preachers deliver
their sermons; the world remains unconverted. According to the
popular belief, current towards the end of the fourteenth century,
no one, since the beginning of the great Western schism, had
entered Paradise.

Thus says Huizinga, in *The Waning of the Middle Ages*.[3] It is a
comfort for us to know we are not the first generation in
history to experience this kind of Apocalyptic disquiet and
dissatisfaction with the existing order. This chronic insecurity,
so like our own in many ways, extended right into the religious
domain, and Eckhart himself was caught up in it, as is seen
in his trial and condemnation. The ground and cause of his
condemnation also bring him close to us. When the official
religious power loses its credibility, various fringe-groups and
marginal movements tend to grow up, especially among the
laity. It seems to have been largely his success with laypeople
that brought down on him the envy and hostility of the church
authorities, and his ultimate condemnation. So when he talks,
as he frequently does, of detachment from time and space,
from the turbulent forces of history, this is not because he
has never experienced these forces himself.

But where did he gain his experience and knowledge of the
inner life, which is the core of his teaching, and the most
precious thing he has to communicate? Here we are faced
with mystery and can only speculate. Something happened
to him, to lead him into the depths of himself and to his final
'breakthrough' – that is clear – but what it was we shall
probably never know. It would help if he talked more about
himself and his own experiences, but he almost never does.
Only on two brief occasions does he seem to refer to something
which he might have been through himself.

The first of these is in a sermon where he says: 'It seemed
to a man as in a dream – it was a waking dream – that he
became pregnant with Nothing, like a woman with child. And

3. Pp. 28–9.

in the Nothing God was born: He was the fruit of Nothing.'[4]
He seems to be referring here to some experience of mystical
death and rebirth; but is it his own or someone else's? We
cannot know for certain.

The second occasion occurs in the *Talks of Instruction*, where
he explains how even sin can sometimes have a good outcome,
in that it leads us to the awareness of our own weakness and
to a greater dependence on God. He then remarks, in passing,
as an illustration: 'Even now one rarely hears of people
achieving great things *unless they first stumble in some respect.*'[5]
Jung, in some ways a very penetrating reader of Eckhart,
attached great weight to this seemingly casual remark. In his
view, casual remarks are often the most significant, since they
betray deep contents of the unconscious mind. That wondrous
poise, buoyancy and spiritual depth so evident in Eckhart,
must, in Jung's view, have involved at some stage a descent
into the darker regions of the inner mind, a confrontation
with all that is most chaotic and destructive in oneself. There
is nothing we can say to this, except that it is speculative.
Perhaps Jung is right, and Eckhart is alluding here to some
'confrontation with the shadow', in the Jungian sense, which
occurred on his way to inner wholeness, but we shall probably
never know. All that we can be sure of is that Eckhart speaks
out of the heart of his own experience, whatever it was.
Every page of his writings shows him as one who speaks with
authority, and 'not as the scribes'.

Perhaps we feel ready, now, to set forth on our spiritual
journey, under the guidance of Meister Eckhart. But before
we do, there is something we must bear in mind. There are
two quite different paths to our spiritual goal, and only one
of them is Eckhart's. Whether we choose his path, or the
other, will depend upon our own temperament and natural
bent.

If, as many have done, we compare the spiritual journey
to the ascent of a mountain, the two paths appear in this
way: the first is a winding path, approaching the summit
gradually, pausing at each stage. It is slow, but thorough.
The second assaults the summit directly, ascending the steep

4. Walshe (see Bibliography, p. 132), vol. 1, no. 19.
5. Clark and Skinner (see Bibliography, p. 132), p. 81.

rock-face without hesitation or delay. The descent afterwards
may be slow and gradual, but the initial ascent is not. It is
a dangerous path, but it attains its goal and is right for those
who are suited to it.

The first path is that of much modern psychoanalysis,
perhaps especially of the Freudian and Jungian type. The
penetration of the deeper levels of the mind, the filtering
through into consciousness of the contents of the unconscious
mind, is slow and gradual. As the unconscious reveals itself
through dreams and symbols, and through impulses never
experienced previously, none of these 'revelations' are
dismissed or discarded. They are to be pondered over,
accepted and worked through gradually, though without
letting ourselves be trapped or overwhelmed by them. If we
patiently and persistently follow this serpentine path into the
depths of ourselves, we shall discover, at the cost of some
danger, unsuspected sources of energy for good or for ill –
buried treasures, guarded by 'dragons' and 'gnomes'; and
if we follow the path right to the end, beyond the merely
psychological, we shall finally come to the deepest level of all,
the 'treasure hidden in the field' of which the gospel speaks –
the pure, undifferentiated consciousness, stripped of all that
is egotistical and personal, the central core of our nature,
where the light of God shines.

This path is not only taken by psychiatry. It is taught and
practised, seemingly, in certain schools of Tantric Buddhism
and, also, it seems, has been trodden by certain Christian
mystics of the visionary and imaginative type, such as Julian
of Norwich and Henry Suso, for whom the revelation of God
comes through visions, symbols thrown up from the deep
levels of the mind, which are meditated on until their meaning
has been extracted.

This is a great path, but it is not the path of Eckhart.

His approach, like that of Zen, perhaps, is direct. It aims
straight for the goal, the deepest layer of the mind, the pure
essence of consciousness which is the Image of God in us. If,
as we penetrate further towards the centre, images and
symbols arise, promises of new desires and new possibilities,
they are to be ignored and passed by, until the Central Core
is reached, where we can become rooted and grounded in
God. Then, strengthened and enlightened by that, we can

ascend slowly to the light, unlocking caverns and treasures on our way, if that seems right. But the first prerequisite is to find God in the deepest core of ourselves, and this is done by detachment, by letting go of all in us that is not God, until a spark of awareness awakens in us, which Eckhart calls 'the Birth of God in the soul'. There is nothing final or definitive about it; it is only a start. There remains the ascent, the gradual exploring of all that was previously neglected. As this process goes on, the spark of consciousness steadily grows until it gradually illuminates the whole mind. It is the work of a lifetime.

This is the path of apophatic mysticism, as taught and practised by Evagrius, by the anonymous author of *The Cloud of Unknowing*, and by all spiritual teachers within that tradition. This is the path which Eckhart outlines in his sermons and treatises.

It is a path which is right for many people, in an age of darkness and confusion. Therefore we can speak of it, in the title of this chapter, as 'Light in the Darkness'. The darkness is not only the insecurity and peril of the present age; it is also the darkness which is within ourselves. The Light is not merely guidance and help in solving our problems in the external world; it is the dawning within us of the awareness of God.

If this path of Eckhart's interests us, then we may proceed. The first thing we have to learn is how to open what is often called today the Wisdom-Eye, but which St Paul calls 'the Eye of the Heart'. In other words, we have to learn a new way of *knowing*. This is the subject of the next chapter.

2 The Eye of the Heart

If we read Eckhart for any length of time, we shall soon become aware of an immense energy, an immense passion, in him. He grips, compels, fascinates; there is nothing cold or dead about him. Yet this passion, this wonderful spiritual drive which animates him, has nothing soft or sentimental about it. It is cool, radiant, light and airy. It has great purity and clarity, like a mountain stream, and it refreshes. How can a passion which is so strong be also so clear and pure? Passion, even spiritual passion, is for us usually a rather muddy affair, the very antithesis of purity. How many of us, when we try to pray or raise our minds to spiritual matters, are put off by the appalling sentimentality of much religious art – pictures, statues, hymns? We can sometimes feel that we would be closer to God in the open air and sunlight, on a breezy mountain-top, than in church, where the atmosphere is either dead and lifeless, or heavy with oppressive, dark emotion.

Yet what we find in Eckhart – the spiritual vision out of which he speaks to us, does suggest the open air and the freely blowing wind. There is something about his way of looking at spiritual matters, of approaching the mystery of God, which is very different from what we are used to. If we are attracted by it and gravitate towards it, that is surely because it is something we need, something we are short of, like a missing vitamin in our diet.

This angle of vision, which makes spiritual truths appear in such fresh and bright colours, is what tinges and character- izes the teaching he is giving us. It is what he is inviting us to share in. If we try to find a single phrase to describe it, we would say, perhaps, that what he is inviting us to do is to open the Wisdom-Eye, the Eye of the Heart.

He is inviting us not merely to *believe* in God, or even to *love* God, though he takes it for granted that we are already trying to do both; what he calls on us to do is to *know* God. He is pointing out to us a new way of *knowing*, and suggesting that we try it.

It is this habit of approaching God through knowledge, the Eye of the Heart, that gives Eckhart that purity and clarity I have spoken of. It gives his vision the coolness and impersonality of a mathematical theorem, yet coupled with immense dynamism and power. We must try to understand this manner of approach, and share it a little, if we are to follow his spiritual path.

Some may feel that it is right to approach God through faith and love, but that to try to approach him through *knowledge* is futile, and even, perhaps, impious. Yet Eckhart did not invent this spiritual path himself, neither was he the first to talk about it. There is plenty about it in Scripture. The prophets, especially, frequently urge us to learn to 'know the Lord'. So there must be a kind of knowledge which really can reach out to God. Eckhart makes it his primary concern, and that is why, when at the University of Paris, he debated so vigorously the question of how we can unite most closely with God – through the Will, by Love, or through the Intellect, by Knowledge. The kind of knowledge he has in mind does not cancel out faith or love; it crowns and perfects them. It is to faith and love what the flower is to the root.

The trouble is, we have too restricted an idea of what it means to *know*. Throughout the greater part of our lives we walk about blindly and mechanically, half asleep, using only about a quarter of the natural power we have been given. There is a knowledge of things which lie beyond anything we can see, hear, smell, touch, taste or imagine; a knowledge which can be raised up to God himself. Such perceptions are not meant to be the prerogative of a privileged minority, composed of theologians, philosophers, monks or ascetics. They are part of that basic human nature which is common to us all; for them to awaken, all that is needed is our desire and co-operation. God himself will do the rest.

But we, as human beings, are capable of several different kinds and levels of knowing. We shall need to glance at a few of these in turn, to find out which is the one which Eckhart is interested in, which is the one that can be raised up to God.

For us today, when we talk about knowledge, we usually mean knowledge of *facts*. I know, for example, that the capital of France is Paris, that the earth circles round the sun. Knowledge of facts is often related to practical skills, which is why it is basic for science and technology. Knowledge of facts, and the acquisition of practical skill, together make up by far the greater part of what we call 'education'. A well-educated man, a man who knows a lot, is one who has at his command a large body of information – not all of it useful information, by any means! – and also a certain amount of technical and practical 'knowhow' which enables him to do certain jobs swiftly and efficiently. Can this kind of practical knowledge and acquisition of information grasp the reality of God? Hardly. He cannot be perceived by the senses, manipulated or controlled by machinery; we cannot get hold of the kind of concrete information about him that might be fed into a computer.

Knowledge of God does not mean knowledge of facts, whether useful or otherwise. Neither does it mean the acquiring of practical skills. So it is not this kind of knowledge which Eckhart is calling us to.

There is another kind of knowledge, which is more abstract. By pondering and meditating on what we percieve of the world through our bodily senses, and on what we have learned to do in a practical way, we can start to *theorize* and *speculate*. We establish links between the various pieces of information we have received, we start to see new connections between them, other possible ways of combining them. In all of this *imagination* plays a large part, and also *memory*. We cannot juggle with and rearrange our sense-given information unless we are able to form pictures of it in our minds (imagination) or to retain it in our minds (memory). We also need to be able to draw conclusions from what we have learned, and see what it implies. That involves the ability to reason *logically*. Memory, imagination and logical reasoning are the prime factors in this kind of abstract knowledge.

It is by knowing in this way that we are able to develop the various sciences, theoretical and practical. We can also go a step further in abstraction, and speculate about the nature of the universe, of man, of perception, being and so on. That leads us to philosophy. Can science or philosophy grasp the reality of God? Hardly. They might lead us to put forward an intellectual theory about God, his existence, nature and properties. But theories about God are not knowledge of God. When the Hebrew prophet said 'Learn to know the Lord', it does not seem likely that he was talking about science or philosophy.

But neither was he talking about theology; and that may surprise us. But if we think for a minute we shall see that in the final analysis theology is not much better equipped to grasp God than science or philosophy. Theology has a certain advantage in that it sets to work on information which God has given us himself, information in which he *reveals* himself to us, through inspired Scriptures, through the teaching, guidance and worship of the Church. But it works on this information in the same way that science and philosophy do; by means of imagination, memory and logic. It works by *distancing* itself from its object, by *abstracting* from it. Can we know God truly in this way? No, because this only tells us things *about* God, it does not bring us into contact with God himself. It gives us information, but not the reality itself.

God cannot be grasped by the senses, nor by the logical, abstracting mind which works on the senses. There has to be a higher kind of knowing which has nothing to do with the senses or the ideas and deductions drawn from them; a knowing which will touch the Reality of God, not merely give information about him, a knowing which casts aside sense impressions and logical deductions, to reach out to God as he really is.

This is what Eckhart himself has to say about the different kinds of knowing:

The first is knowledge of creatures, which we can perceive through the five senses, and all things which are objective to man. In these we do not know God properly, for they are coarse. The second knowledge is more spiritual, and we can have it with the absent, as when I know a friend a thousand miles away whom I have previously seen. But I must see him in likeness (i.e. in imagination), his dress, his form and time and place. That too is crude and material. With this knowledge one cannot know God: one cannot know Him by time or place or appearance. The third . . . is purely spiritual knowledge; therein the soul is rapt away from all objective bodily things. There we hear without any sound and see without matter: there is neither white nor black nor red . . . Speaking of this knowledge, St John says: 'That light enlightens all who come into this world.'[1]

We in the modern world have a great deal of the lower kinds of knowledge: factual, practical, scientific, philosophical, theological. But the highest knowledge, the only one capable of touching God, is very rare. Few people know what it is like, some would doubt its possibility, many would deny it outright. The lower forms of knowledge, which are so familiar to us, are not merely incapable of reaching God, they actually blot him out, prevent the knowledge of him from dawning in our minds. This is because they work upon the senses, and upon information derived from the senses. But the senses are bound to the world of space and time, and God is above space and time. Sense-knowledge – at least at the opening of our spiritual journey – impedes the awareness of God. We have to drop it, and the imagination and logic derived from it. When sense-impressions, images and ideas have been cast aside, then the knowledge of God can shine forth. We have to renounce all that we normally call 'knowledge' if we wish to attain to this higher kind.

At first this looks rather daunting. We can begin to see now why in the first chapter Eckhart appeared as the intrepid climber who makes the direct assault upon the summit, straight up the rock-face, rather than taking the meandering, winding path. But if we give way to panic, this is because we are seeing the ascent to knowledge in a merely negative way, in terms of what has to be renounced and abandoned. We are overlooking the fact that this high knowledge also has its positive side. It has its own magnetism, its own power of attraction, which will draw us upwards of itself, if we only let it.

We shall look now at some of these more attractive and 'magnetic' aspects to the Path of Knowledge.

First of all, it is not a knowledge which works indirectly, reasoning logically on the basis of information received. It is direct, immediate, intuitive. Knower and known are united

1. Walshe, vol. 2, pp. 213–14.

in an instantaneous flash of illumination; nothing is allowed to intervene or mediate between them. One of Eckhart's favourite terms for this kind of knowledge is *ohne mittel* ('unmediated' or 'im-mediate'); in other words, not indirect and logical, but direct and intuitive.

Such knowledge is by no means beyond our reach. It is not necessarily mystical or supernatural; there are less exalted forms of it which are part of our daily experience. We may have a direct perception, for example, of what someone else is thinking, or planning to do, even though no word has been spoken and no sign given. We may sense, with unerring certainty, that some particular event is about to occur, or is already occurring now, although there is nothing perceptible to suggest this. These are simple, everyday examples of the workings of the higher, intuitive intellect, which grasps its object directly. But it can also grasp spiritual objects directly, and even God himself, when it has been sufficiently prepared and God has given the grace.

The second thing to notice about this kind of knowledge is that it is based upon *communion* and *likeness*. In other words, we only truly know in this sense when we *unite* with that which we know, become one with it, and thus come also to *resemble* it. The idea that we can only know in the deepest sense through communion is not an invention of Eckhart's. Obviously he possessed this kind of knowledge himself to a very high degree, and he could, if he wanted, have been content simply to enjoy it. But the joy and energy which came to him through it led him to want to share it with others, and to try to find some viable language in which to explain it. He found this language in two sources: the Bible, which was the supreme spiritual authority of his day, and the writings of Aristotle, which were the supreme philosophical authority of his day.

The truth that knowledge, in the deepest sense, means communion, is constantly affirmed in the Bible. When the Book of Genesis, for example, tells us that Adam 'knew' Eve his wife, it is not talking about scientific, philosophical, or theological knowledge. It is talking about knowledge through communion, in this case communion of the flesh, consummated by a man and a woman within a marital relationship. But the same word, 'knowledge', is often used to refer to

communion with God as well. When the prophets talk of
'knowing' the Lord, this, again, has nothing to do with
science, philosophy, or theology. It refers to a concrete flesh-
and-blood relationship, which includes all aspects of life. In
this relationship, this 'knowledge', Israel, the Chosen People,
becomes the Bride of Jahweh, and through this union with
him becomes also to a certain extent like him, sharing in his
glory and splendour, as a bride is adorned in fine garments
and jewels.

As for what Aristotle has to say about knowledge as
communion, we need not go into this too deeply, save to
notice that he seems to have thought that *all* knowledge is of
this kind. We are not obliged to agree with him. Is it really
true, for example, that I cannot know a pencil, unless I
become one with it, and come in some degree to resemble it?
But this is irrelevant; for even though we may disagree with
Aristotle when he suggests that *all* knowledge involves
communion and likeness, we shall have no difficulty in recognizing that there are many cases in our own experience when
knowledge does take this form. We may even say, perhaps,
that the truest and deepest knowledge tends to take this form
inevitably, by a kind of inexorable law. Everyday life provides
us with plenty of examples. A man or woman, for instance,
who works a lot with horses, who comes to understand them
very well, may come to acquire a number of horse-like
features, in appearance and behaviour! And how can anyone
teach or work with children, and come to know and love
them, unless he has something of the child in his own
character? Again, deep human relationships, such as a
marriage or an intimate friendship, in which the partners
claim to truly know each other – do they not involve an
exchange of characteristics, so that the partners come
progressively to resemble each other? Even relationships of
hostility and aggression can assume this character provided
they are sufficiently intense, and the parties concerned are
sufficiently committed and involved in the relationship. A
wrestler, or a boxer, has to come to *know* his opponent, to get
inside his mind, to think and feel as he does, in order to be
able to overthrow him. A hunter, too, has to *become* the animal
he stalks, putting aside his own human thoughts and reactions, so as to know how to bring the animal down. The

boundary line between love and hate can be very narrow on these occasions, even, perhaps, vanishing altogether at times, so that we can say that the hunter *loves* his quarry, and the warrior his enemy . . . that the husband *hates* his wife and the teacher his pupils . . . The important thing is that the relationship should be sufficiently intense to generate knowledge by communion and likeness. Differences between the partners may remain, but there must be some point where they are one.

Jacob and Job come to know the Lord, to unite with him and resemble him, by wrestling with him intently in the darkness. Knower and known often have to experience the clash of their difference and separateness, in order to find their ground of union and likeness.

Knowledge of God, then, means union with God, a kind of union which leads us to actually *resemble* God in some measure, to become to a certain extent like him. It is something which the Scriptures themselves call upon us to attempt. 'You, therefore, must be perfect,' says Jesus, 'as your heavenly Father is perfect.'

It is a lofty and sublime aim, but not beyond our reach. On the contrary, it is something which we are meant for; the only thing which in the end will bring us real fulfilment. We may feel tempted to draw back and say 'Oh no, these dizzy heights are not for me. They are only for those especially favoured people whom God lifts up to them. I can't possibly expect to climb so high by my puny efforts'. But this, in Eckhart's view, is false humility. It is true that the high knowledge is a gift from God, which he is free to give or withhold as he wills. But the fact is that he *wants* to bestow it on us; he is constantly watching and waiting for his chance to give it to us. The only thing that prevents him is our unwillingness and unreadiness to receive. Once we are ready, God will act immediately, and rush in to flood our whole being with his glory and power.

The goal of Divine Knowledge, then, is high; but not unattainable. We shall attain it, if we truly desire it, even though everything depends upon that 'if'.

It is also what we all desire already, whether we are fully aware of this or not. A text which Eckhart is specially fond of quoting is from the *Confessions* of St Augustine: ' . . . Thou

hast made us for Thyself, O God, and our hearts are restless
until they rest in Thee.' The thirst for God, the desire for
unitive knowledge, is not something foreign to our nature,
therefore needing to be artificially stimulated, as commercial
advertising seeks to awaken desires and needs in us which we
never had before. This desire, on the contrary, is there already
in the human heart; the only reason we fail to perceive it is
because it is usually covered up with rubbish, with petty
worries and egotistical ambitions. Once these are removed,
the true desire, buried in the deepest recesses of the human
mind, will shine forth of itself and, like a flame, will leap up
towards Heaven, which is its true home.

> . . . God's image, the Son of God, is in the ground of the soul
> like a living fountain. But if anyone throws earth, that is, earthly
> desire upon it, it is impeded and covered up, so that one cannot
> recognize anything of it or be aware of it. Yet it remains living
> in itself, and when the earth that has been thrown upon it from
> outside is taken away, it appears and one becomes aware of it.
> And he [Origen] says that this truth is exemplified in the First
> Book of Moses, in which it is written that Abraham had dug
> living wells in his field, and evil-doers filled them with earth; but
> later when the earth was thrown out, the wells flowed again.[2]

A natural desire for the infinite and perfect, which God will
certainly answer, once it is awake; a desire for a union with
God so close that we actually begin to resemble him, and
take on some of his characteristics – such is the Divine Knowledge which is the goal of the path which Eckhart invites us
to tread. It is easy to see that there is nothing cold or unfeeling
about knowledge of this sort. It is ardent and fiery, though
very pure. It is grounded upon faith and love, since it involves
the giving of oneself totally; it involves surrender. For if we
ponder for a moment, we shall see that faith is not merely a
notional assent to what we are told about God through the
Scriptures or the Church; as if we were to recite the Apostles'
Creed, say 'I believe' to it all, then go away and forget all
about it. True faith involves commitment and surrender, a
leap into the darkness, believing that there we shall find God.
Love, too, is essentially about commitment and surrender,
and the desire for union. Yielding, surrendering to the

2. Clark and Skinner, pp. 152–3.

magnetic attraction of God, casting aside all that might hinder our union with him; this is what faith and love are all about, and this is what leads us to the Wisdom of the Heart, the true knowledge of God.

How, then, does this knowledge differ from faith and love? Is it not just another name for the same thing, the same act of surrender? Almost, but not quite. Knowledge differs from faith and love in only one respect: by being more concentrated and intense, and thus coming closer to its goal. It pierces through all the veils which hide its object and penetrates to the Reality behind, pure and naked. It will not be satisfied with a revelation of God, or a reflection of God's glory; it wants God himself, the Reality which is partly revealed, but also partly concealed, in what is communicated to us through words, symbols, created things. It catches God off his guard, naked, 'in his dressing-room', as Eckhart puts it.

It also annihilates all distinction, all separateness, and rests only in perfect unity. In love, however close the union and communion, the two partners always remain to some extent separate; there is always 'I' and 'You'. But knowledge is not content with this; it is not satisfied with a state of communion and likeness; it wants to press on further until there is no more 'I' and 'You' but only Oneness. It is no longer merely *like* God, it has *become* God. This is how Eckhart himself describes it:

> The soul is one with God and not united. Here is a simile: if we fill a tub with water, the water in the tub is united but not one with it, for where there is water there is no wood, and where there is wood there is no water. Now take the wood and throw it in the middle of the water; still the wood is only united and not one (with the water). It is different with the soul: she becomes one with God and not united, for where God is, there the soul is and where the soul is, there God is.
>
> Scripture says: 'Moses saw God face to face' (Ex 33:11). The masters deny this,[3] saying where two faces appear God is not seen, for God is one and not two: for whoever sees God sees nothing but one.[4]

Knowledge is this fiery longing for oneness with God, cutting

---

3. I.e. deny that the literal meaning of this phrase is sufficient as it stands.
4. Walshe, vol. 2, p. 225.

through all veils and all distinctions. It differs from faith and love only in that it raises them to their maximum concentration and intensity, to a kind of distilled quintessence. Now we see why it is that Eckhart's spirituality has this extraordinary purity and radiance; all impurities have been smelted out by the heat of spiritual longing, and all that remains is the white, incandescent light of Divine Knowledge.

> God guard me from those thoughts men think
> In the mind alone;
> He that sings a lasting song
> Thinks in a marrow-bone.

Thus wrote the poet W. B. Yeats, expressing his conviction that the truest knowledge and deepest wisdom can never be something of the brain only, but must emanate from the core of the *whole* human being, flesh and blood, bone, marrow and sinew. This is why we have chosen to call it 'the Eye of the Heart' – not only because this term was used by St Paul and the early Church Fathers, but also because it shows that knowledge is not something pale and bloodless, but rather expresses all that is most central and vital in us.

We now have some notion of what our spiritual goal is. To finish off this chapter, we need to see something of how it will look and feel in actual practice. I have called Eckhart's way 'the Way of Paradox', because he sees the Reality of God as something that can be grasped only within the tension and clash of opposites. This tension has to be experienced in our daily life; this is the practice of *detachment*. But it also has to be experienced in our thinking and talking about God; and this involves *paradox*.

A good way of getting used to this idea is to glance at the beginning of a sermon in which Eckhart outlines his 'programme' for preaching:

> When I preach, it is my wont to speak about detachment, and of how man should rid himself of self and all things. Secondly, that man should be reinformed back into the simple good which is God. Thirdly, that we should remember the great nobility God has put into the soul, so that man may come miraculously to God. Fourthly, of the purity of the divine nature, for the splendour of God's nature is unspeakable.[5]

5. Walshe, vol. 1, p. 177.

In other words, he begins with *practice*, telling us how we must live our everyday lives if the knowledge of God is to dawn in us. This is the practice of detachment, which I shall describe in more detail later on. But for the moment we shall look at the other points in Eckhart's 'programme'. We shall see at once that they are all special *themes* in the spiritual life, which he regards as essential, and which we must concentrate on if we are to reach our goal. When he says that we should be 'reinformed back into . . . God', he is pointing out the goal itself, which is to make the steep, rapid ascent to God, like a mountaineer scaling a lofty peak, to the point when we and God are one, when we regain that unity which we are destined for. Next he points out the natural sublimity of the human heart, which makes it really possible for us to ascend these heights. Lastly, he recalls the goal again in all its splendour, so as to kindle our desire.

But this is only the surface meaning. There is far more here than a simple programme for preaching. And despite the fact that it presents us with a number of 'themes' in the spiritual life, there is more to it than a simple exposition of doctrine. On the contrary; if we look closer we shall find that this passage has a certain 'icon-like' quality, in that it is not meant simply to teach a doctrine but also to kindle a certain kind of awareness. In other words, we can profitably use it as a support for meditation and prayer, because if we ponder over it slowly and carefully, letting its phrases resound in the mind, we shall begin to have a glimmering awareness of a world beyond that in which we normally live. This effect, which we might almost call 'poetic' and 'magical', is due to Eckhart's special way of thinking and of using language. It is this which enables him not merely to *talk* about spiritual realities, but at the same time to kindle in his listeners an awareness that these realities truly exist, that we have only to reach out in order to be able to touch them. Things which previously we had only heard or read about, now begin actually to impinge on our consciousness, and the spiritual quest emerges as something possible and eminently desirable.

We need to learn this way of thinking and speaking about spiritual truths, so typical of Eckhart, because our own spiritual lives will then be refreshed by it. The thing to grasp about it is that it is founded on *antithesis* and *paradox*, the contrast and clash between opposites. We see this clearly in the quoted extract on page 24. It begins with practical counsel about how we live in the world we actually find ourselves in, dominated by 'self' and 'all things' which we have to detach from. Then it swings right away from the earthly pole of existence and plunges us into the Mystery of God, with whom we hope to unite. Then we are swung back into our own world again, and plunged into the human world, to explore the depths of our own souls, where there is a great treasure waiting to be uncovered. Finally, we are lifted out of the human world and plunged again into the depths of God, the abyss of mystery which is his nature. This swinging rhythm or oscillation between unlike poles, breathing in and breathing out, speaking and remaining silent, doing and resting, is the basic rhythm of the spiritual life, and it is only within that rhythm that we can know God, experience him, think and talk about him. If we abandon ourselves to this rhythm, let ourselves be carried by it, it will gradually kindle within us the spark of Divine Knowledge. It will open for us the Wisdom-Eye, the Eye of the Heart.

That is why we call the way taught by Eckhart the Way of Paradox, because it is founded on the tension between opposites. If the Eye of the Heart were fully open, and we had attained complete Divine Knowledge, we would see that these contraries are all contained finally in an all-embracing *unity*; God and Man, pleasure and pain, success and failure, are ultimately all one in God. But we cannot reach this perception save in and through the tension of opposites. That is why Cardinal Nicholas of Cusa, a profound thinker and enthusiastic reader of Eckhart, came to conceive God as the *coincidentia oppositorum*, the coming together of opposites.

This tension has to be experienced on two levels: first, in daily living; second, in thought and speech. Another word for it is *crucifixion*, for the Cross is the perfect symbol of the tension between opposites, and the all-embracing unity in which they are reconciled. In daily living, the tension is experienced as detachment, the crucifixion of the will. But there also has to be a crucifixion of *thought* and *speech*. The idea that mind and language have to be crucified may strike us as rather strange at first; but if we pause for a moment we shall see that it must be so. I am destined for union with God; I was created for that; and will find fulfilment only in that. But I cannot attain this by remaining what I am now; I have to die somehow to the life I am living, so as to find the new life in God. This death and rebirth must involve my *whole* self, not only my daily life, but also my thought and speech. No part of me, not even my mind and tongue, can get through to God without passing through the clash of contraries.

That is why Eckhart talks constantly in antitheses and paradoxes. The deepest truth of God can be grasped only in this way. Therefore, in his preaching and writing, Eckhart keeps us perpetually swinging from one pole to the other; he will not let us rest in either. To rest in one and forget the other is to lose hold of the truth, which is essentially paradoxical. God is everything, yet nothing; distinct from creation, yet indistinct from it; there is a tension between action and contemplation, withdrawal and involvement, silence and speech, being and nothingness. Having made a statement, Eckhart will often go on to deny it; but the truth lies neither in the affirmation nor in the denial, but in the tug-of-war between the two. This is baffling for the normal human mind, which works on the logical Principle of Contradiction, according to which a proposition cannot be both true and false at one and the same time. But according to Eckhart, that is exactly what the highest truth is. It transcends the Principle of Contradiction, and can be grasped only through paradox.

This way of opening the Wisdom-Eye through paradox and the clash of contraries will remind many people of Zen; and indeed there is a certain similarity, though Eckhart's way is totally Christian, founded on the mystery of the cross and the resurrection, in which the perception of unity in the clash of opposites is realized to the highest degree. Yet the radiance and the lightness of touch in Eckhart are reminiscent of Zen. The purpose of paradox, too, is the same in both cases: it is not to deny or destroy the human mind with nonsense but to bring the normal human intellect to the awareness of its own limitations, and thus open it up to the possibility of a higher kind of knowing. If we accept this, and follow Eckhart in his Way of Paradox, we shall obtain a glimpse of that knowledge which was his. If we view the Christian Revelation and seek to live it, in accordance with this Way, we shall find that many

mysteries will be unlocked for us and our whole spiritual life
will be energized. I shall try to point the way to this in the
chapters which follow.

3   The Silent Desert

Once the Eye of the Heart is open, and trained on its goal, the spiritual seeker is confronted with the question: what are you looking for? The Christian will then reply: God. But this answer is not enough for the spiritual intellect, for it simply calls forth the further question: what, for you, is God?

For Eckhart, this is the fundamental question; everything hangs upon it. It is by no means merely academic, of interest only to the professional theologian or the philosopher; it is the very stuff and fibre of the spiritual life. The way we approach it, and the kind of answer we make to it, will determine the whole character and direction of our life from now on, because whatever we may think or say on the theoretical level, in actual hard fact 'God' is simply another word for 'reality' and 'goal'. My 'God' is, in practice, that which my whole life tends towards, that which for me is most *real*. Officially and nominally, I may be a Christian, that is to say, a believer in the transcendent God revealed in the Bible and preached by the Church. But if my life is, in actual fact, dedicated to something else, as, for example, making money; if for me money, and what are called 'economic facts', is what truly counts; if in the deepest core of myself I believe that money is the greatest and most effective power in the world – then my God is money, even though I may cheerfully stand up in church on Sunday morning and recite the Nicene Creed, thinking that I believe in it.

A person attempting to live a serious spiritual life may not find it too difficult to recognize and reject idolatry, when it takes obvious and gross forms such as the thirst for money, or power, or sensual pleasure. But there are more subtle forms, much harder to recognize, because they are so much closer to the real thing and therefore so much more easily confused with it. Christianity is a religion based on revelation, on the belief that God communicates himself to us in tangible, recognizable forms: the Church, liturgy, Scripture, sacraments, dogmas, religious orders and societies, different kinds of pastoral and apostolic activity. It may be true that God is present in these things, and reveals himself in them and through them. But are they actually God himself? Obviously not; indeed, so obviously not, that one might wonder if there is any point in asking the question at all. But there is a vast difference between understanding the distinction in theory and actually realizing it in practice. In practice, we tend to cling to one or several of the various forms in which God has revealed himself, as if they were the end rather than the means; the goal rather than the path leading to the goal. Yet this, too, is idolatry, and the genuine spiritual intellect, once awake, will have none of it. The God revealed in Christ and preached by Eckhart is a transcendent God; he is not any one of the finite, limited things he has made, however good or holy they may be. God is not anything that can be grasped by the senses, pictured by the imagination, understood by the mind. As Eckhart often puts it, 'God is neither this not that'. If we have obtained something, experienced something, understood something, that may be good and of great value, but it is not God. Since it is not God, we have to be very careful not to treat it as if it were.

To accept and worship God in his transcendence is not at all as common a thing as we might think. It requires great courage because it means a leap into the void, it means abandoning things which are familiar, safe, secure. Not everyone sees the value of that, or the need for it. But it has some advantages, which it may be worth our while to consider briefly before we go further.

The first is the lure of mystery. If we are honest with ourselves, we have to admit that the mysterious, the unfathomable, the intangible, has a certain magnetic fascination – accompanied by some fear and dread, perhaps, but still compelling in its attractiveness. In touching God, we are touching upon the supremely mysterious. To say 'God' is to say that at the heart of the world we live in, the world of people and things, there lies an unfathomable mystery; when the scientists, philosophers, theologians and artists have said all the profound things they are able to say, there remains something unsaid – and unsayable. There is something refreshing about this fact. Great though Shakespeare, Newton and St Thomas Aquinas may be, it would be stifling and deadening if their sublime utterances contained the *whole* truth, if there were no reality beyond. When St Thomas Aquinas, towards the end of his life, had a mystical glimpse of the true nature of God, it led him to see all his previous voluminous writings on theology as 'straw'; yet there is no hint that this was a depressing discovery for him. On the contrary it brought a sense of relief and joy. That which is holy must also be inviolate – something that cannot be debased by glib talk, cannot be controlled, abused, manipulated. To say that at the heart of the world lies a mystery, is to glimpse the possibility that it may have some kind of ultimate meaning; that it may, after all, be worthwhile.

The second attraction of the transcendent God is the lure of adventure. A transcendent God is one who cannot be pinned down, controlled or predicted. To cast oneself into the transcendent God is to cast oneself into the unknown. Religion withers at the heart when it becomes too domesticated, when its God has become tame, docile, and entirely safe. The God of Abraham was not like that, nor the God of Moses, still less the God whom Jesus addressed as 'Father' – to serve their God was to embark upon an adventure, in which almost anything might happen. Safety and security have their own appeal, but on their own they cannot fully satisfy. Most people have in them at least a streak of the spirit of adventure, which led St Augustine to say of himself, as a young man, that he hated security 'and a path with no snares for my feet'.

The third attraction of the transcendent God is the lure of truth. This is perhaps the most important of all, and to feel this kind of attraction is one of the clearest signs that spiritual intelligence is awake in us. One of the most devastating blows to religious faith during the last 200 years or so has been the growing suspicion that our 'God' is simply an invention of our own, a 'projection', as the psychologists would say, a fantasy conjured up by our own imagination to enable us to face a world which, if we saw it as it really is, would be meaningless, bleak, arid and intolerable. Hence the famous saying: 'If God did not exist, then it would be necessary to invent him' – which leaves us with the suspicion that we *have* invented him, fabricated him out of our own need. But it was perhaps Freud, above all, in *The Future of an Illusion*, who most openly denounced religion as a mere projection of our subconscious hopes and fears, a comforting dream conjured up by our imagination to compensate for our unresolved psychological complexes. The same insinuation is present in Jung, despite his much greater respect for religion and his immense appreciation of its value; one senses that for him the 'gods' of the various religions are pure inventions of the human mind, images superimposed upon the real world, rather than a recognition of something which actually exists in its own right. This led him to seriously misunderstand Eckhart in some respects, saying, for example, that in Eckhart the externalized God of traditional Christianity becomes a purely inward, subjective reality. A dangerous mistake, since it is so nearly right, as we shall see later; a mistake which we cannot afford to make, if we are to understand Eckhart's teaching and follow it. His God is emphatically not a projection, however noble, sublime or necessary. For him spiritual life consists precisely in the *withdrawal* of projections, in order to get at what really exists. Spiritual intelligence, as he conceives it, is concerned above all with the truth.

What has this got to do with the transcendence of God? Everything. It is to recognize that Freud and Jung are to a certain extent right; a large part of what we call 'religion' really *is* projection, which means that it says more about us than about God. This has all to be stripped away, if we are to reach our goal, but the stripping has to be gentle and gradual, for the projections do have their own value, even though it may be only a limited one. As we grow into the truth, the projections are cast aside; instead of seeing God as we would like him to be, we come closer to seeing him as he really is. But there have to be projections in the beginning; without them the spiritual life cannot get started. At first our notion of God is distorted by our personal needs and emotions; it takes time for all that to be refined and purified so that the truth may emerge.

Perhaps the whole process becomes easier to understand if we compare it to a profound human relationship, as, for example, a marriage. When a young couple are at the courtship stage, their relationship contains a very large amount of projection. They do not see each other as they really are, but through a rosy haze of emotion which is generated largely by their own inner needs and inadequacies. Each partner appears to the other far more admirable than is really the case. Yet the presence of these projections does not necessarily mean that the relationship is illusory, that there is no real bond linking the two young people together. The bond may be really there; it is merely the true nature of it that the young couple are mistaken about. They have not, as yet, come to distinguish the superficial from the essential, the transitory from the permanent. They think that their 'love' is this heady emotional intoxication that sets their senses reeling; they do not, as yet, understand love as knowing and accepting each other for what they really are, as giving, as sacrifice, as remaining faithful in the face of difficulties and disappointments. As the two of them live together and face the problems of life together, then they gradually, over the years, get to know each other in a much more genuine way; the projections are gradually dropped, and something else emerges which is purer, stronger and more truthful.

But all this takes time; in fact, a lifetime. A young couple cannot be expected to know and accept the truth about each other straight away; at the beginning of the relationship there have to be projections, because without them no emotional heat would be generated sufficient to draw the young people together and enable them to begin to get to know each other, however imperfectly at first. It is in the midst of that crucible of passion that the chemical reaction is set up that welds their lives together, which lays the foundation of a relationship which will still endure when all the fire and molten heat has died down. We cannot assume that a relationship is unreal or illusory simply because it is accompanied in its early stages by projections and emotional excitement. That is the way it has to start. First, the drowsy scent of roses and the heavy fumes of wine; only later comes a fresher, purer air and a clear, brilliant sunlight.

It is the same with that other, much more profound relationship: our relationship with God. At the beginning there are projections, with all the emotional heat associated with them. It has to be this way; otherwise the spiritual life will never get going at all. We call God 'Father' or even 'Mother', as Julian of Norwich did; we attribute to him all kinds of perfections which we find lacking in ourselves, such as wisdom, power, kindness, patience and so on, forgetting that God is in fact not a human being at all, and therefore cannot possibly be fatherly, motherly, wise, powerful, kind or patient in the same way that humans are. But we have to think of him in this way at first, simply to get the relationship going. Once it has started and begun to grow, then the refining and purifying process can begin, whereby the projections are slowly withdrawn and the truth emerges.

This was Freud's mistake: he thought that because religion starts with projection and fantasy, that is all there is to it, and relationship with God is an illusion. It is not, any more than a marriage relationship is illusory simply because it begins with emotional dreams. Truth comes with maturity, in religion as in marriage, and it is the mature relationship, not the youthful one, that we need to examine if we want to assess its degree of genuineness.

Far from being dismayed at the suggestion that religion contains projections, some spiritual teachers have calmly recognized the fact and actually used it as a means of spiritual training. Alexandra David Neel tells of Tibetan lamas, who train their disciples to build up a mental picture of their tutelary deity, putting all their emotional and imaginative strength into it, until the point is reached when this image appears to the disciple as real and as concrete as anything in the world around him – perhaps even *more* real. Then comes the difficult and delicate moment when the teacher awakens the disciple to the illusory nature of what he has built up, to the realization that it is, in fact, *as an image*, a projection of his own mind. This is followed by the slow and painful task of withdrawing the projection, dissolving the image, until the disciple comes to realize that the deity is not without, but within, one with his own mind. The operation is fraught with danger, of course, and requires great skill on the part of the teacher, since when the disciple realizes that he has been projecting, the temptation is for him to think that he was *only* projecting, that his deity has no real existence at all. If he yields to this temptation, he will fall into despair, thinking that his spiritual life has been a total waste of time. It has not. His error lies, not in thinking that his deity exists, but in misunderstanding its true nature, in regarding it as something entirely separate, external, distinct from him, 'out there'. If he continues his training he will soon rediscover his lost deity within himself, and will reach a truer and stabler vision. Nevertheless the early stage, of projection, cannot be dispensed with. The externalized image is needed at the beginning, to awaken the spiritual energy within the disciple, to kindle the sacred fire within his heart, and make him aware – however dimly and imperfectly – of the deity's existence.

This is not fundamentally different from what Eckhart is doing in his teaching on Divine Transcendence, on the God who is 'neither this nor that'. He is taking the average Christian, whose spiritual life has hitherto been based largely on projections, on externalized images, and teaching him to *withdraw* these projections, so that he may come eventually to understand the true nature of his goal. Unless he starts by imagining God as 'out there', and projecting all sorts of human qualities onto him, he will never come to believe in God at all. The art is to withdraw the projection with great care and delicacy, so that what emerges at the end is not a hopeless vacuum but a deeper truth.

Genuine spiritual intellect can be satisfied with nothing less than this. We saw in the preceding chapter how the Eye of the Heart pierces through the images to get at the Reality. In other words, the projections must go. We want a union with God which is, in Eckhart's words, *ohne mittel*, im-mediate, not mediated through an image. We also want a union in which there is no more sense of distinction, of separateness, of 'I' and 'You', but only oneness. Therefore the notion must go of a God who is purely external to us, 'out there'.

Atheism and rationalism strip away the projection and leave us with nothing. That leads to nihilism and despair. Eckhart's Way of Transcendence strips away the projections in such a manner as to unveil the truth behind them. That is life-giving. It is the step from spiritual childhood to maturity; from the 'milk for babes' which St Paul speaks of, to the 'strong meat' which can only be given to those who are ready for it.

The Transcendent God is a truth which can only be realized gradually by a progressive stripping-away of the veils.

The first veil to remove is that of the material world. To say that God is 'neither this nor that' means that we are not to see our goal as anything limited or material, such as money, comfort, pleasure, security, status, the good opinion of others. God is not any of these things; that much should be obvious, however difficult it may be to realize in practice. But neither, says Eckhart, should we identify our God with other things which may be more sublime but are nevertheless limited and creaturely. A person who cannot pray without the assistance of Gregorian Chant, stained-glass windows and Latin, is, in effect, identifying his 'God' with a particular form of liturgy. The same is true of one who demands guitars, a rock group, and exuberant embraces at the Kiss of Peace. These things may be there, or may not be there; we need to learn to take what comes and not be too worrried about what is absent. Eckhart is very ironical about those who are attached to what he calls 'particular ways of devotion'. But there are also particular ways of *life* which we identify with God. A harassed housewife complains that she has too much to do to have time for God; she *would* be religious if she had no family to look after and if she were able to become a contemplative nun or a medical missionary. As it is, she has no chance. Though she may not realize it, she is implying that only monks and nuns are able to seek God, that lay life is irremediably 'profane'. That is not only an insult to lay life, it is also an idolatry of professional religious life, implying that in it alone can God be found and nowhere else. That is what Eckhart means by detachment to particular ways of life.

The second veil to be removed is more inward, concerned with our mental, imaginative and emotional life, especially that area of it which we consider to be 'religious'. In other words, I am speaking now of those activities of ours which are consciously and explicitly directed towards God: reading theology and spiritual books, reflecting on them and discussing them; also our life of prayer and worship, both private and communal. Not everyone spends a great deal of time reading theology or spirituality, but everyone who has any kind of spiritual life at all engages in some form of prayer or worship, so perhaps it would be as well to look at this aspect first. How are we to realize the true, transcendent God in our devotional life?

Eckhart is assuming that we are Catholic Christians, rather than Christians of a purely inward and contemplative type, as, for example, the Quakers. In other words, he is assuming that we belong to a Church which presents God to us in symbolic form, through certain doctrines, hierarchical structures and religious rites. He knows that the Church has very good and legitimate reasons for doing this. One of these is our very nature as human beings: the fact that we have bodies as well as souls; that as a rule we are unable to think or perceive anything without the help of images drawn from the bodily world; and that in any case we need to learn to offer our *whole* selves to God, not just our more angelic and spiritual parts but our bodies as well. Besides, God has already appeared to us himself in human form, in the person of Jesus of Nazareth; since the Incarnation of Christ no one has the right to suggest that the use of religious images is wrong, either in theology or in worship. Before we go any further, we must bear in mind that Eckhart understands all this very well, and is not denying any part of it. He himself was a Dominican friar and priest, bound by his duty to the Church and to his Order, to the daily celebration of Mass and the recitation of the Divine Office. There is no evidence that he was at all lax or careless in his dedication to these duties, or that he encouraged other people to be so. In other words, he made full use of the images and symbols of God which the Church has handed down over the centuries, and had no desire to do away with them. Where he differed from any of his contemporaries, and where he differs from many Christians today lies in his *attitude* towards these traditional images – the kind of *use* he makes of them.

What is this attitude? And what is he calling upon us to do, with regard to these traditional symbols? First of all he wants us to use them to the extent that the Church obliges us to use them, and also to the extent that they are indispensable to our personal spiritual life. We must, for example, go to Mass and frequent the other sacraments, ponder the Scriptures and think about God; the Church obliges us to all this. If, in addition, we find that our personal spiritual life is helped by some optional devotions, such as praying the

Rosary or performing the Stations of the Cross – devotions
which are based upon imagery – then we should not lightly
desist from them. But we should desist from these imaged
devotions which are not of obligation, if we feel the call to do
so, and if we find ourselves drawn to a more inward kind of
prayer which does not use images or concepts, the type shown
sometimes as 'pure' prayer, the type taught by Evagrius and
the author of *The Cloud of Unknowing*. Indeed, an increasingly
conscious need for this type of prayer is one of the clearest
signs of an aptitude for the spiritual way taught by Eckhart.
Even if we practise it for no more than five to ten minutes a
day, that does not matter; the aptitude is nevertheless there,
however small and germinal it may be at present.

But when we do think and pray in images – at Mass, for
example, or in pondering theology – how does Eckhart want
us to do it? He wants us not to discard the images or cast
them aside, but, so to speak, to look through them, look
beyond them to the Reality which they reflect and which we
cannot as yet see. We shall deal with the question of images
in our devotional life in a later chapter, dedicated specifically
to this question. For the moment we should see how we are
to purify our theological life, our thinking and meditating
about God.

Eckhart gives us a lot of help here. Constantly in his
sermons he talks about God in such a way as to shock us into
an awareness of how shallow and inadequate our habitual
notions of God are. We call him a Person, imagining him to
be like the human persons we meet in everyday life; we call
him Spirit, imagining some kind of disembodied ghost; we
call him good and wise, projecting onto him these qualities
which we have seen in people we love and admire. To a
certain extent this is all perfectly valid; it starts our spiritual
life off, and gets it going. But the amount of projection and
illusion in it is colossal. It overlooks the vast gulf which
separates the Creator from his creation. If God really is a
Person, it can only be in a sense very different from what we
normally mean by that term. Similarly, if we call God a
Spirit, or say that he is good and wise, we must understand
that when applied to God these terms must bear a meaning
very different from their normal one. In fact, the difference
is so enormous that we might well ask whether these terms

are applicable at all. Eckhart often shocks us deliberately by suggesting that they are not. 'If I say that God is good,' he says in one sermon, 'that is not true. God is not good; I am good. And if I say that God is wise, that is not true. I am wiser than He is.'

This kind of language is meant to shock, and it does. It is not hard to see why the judges at Cologne and Avignon were dismayed and alarmed. Yet if we let ourselves get over the shock and still give serious consideration to what Eckhart is saying, it becomes liberating and vitalizing. Many grave problems in life – spiritual, psychological and moral – spring from a faulty and incomplete notion of God, often inherited from infancy or early childhood when our attitude to 'God' was inextricably mixed up with our attitude to our parents and teachers. How often a reaction against religious faith, in adult life, is at heart a reaction against an authoritarian father or dominating mother, or a Church which appears as an extension of these! When we start to free ourselves from these infantile dependencies, we may be tempted also to throw away the religion which was associated with them, feeling that we have 'grown out of all that'. But this is a mistake. We may no longer want the God of our childhood; but that does not necessarily mean we should have no God at all. Genuine spiritual growth means that our concepts of God will be undergoing continual change and transformation throughout life; we shall not rest content with any one of them, but always be prepared to move on when we are ready, recognizing that in the final analysis *no* concept of God is adequate to the Reality, and the Reality will only dawn in its fullness when our life has run its entire course.

'God is not good. God is not wise.' That is to say, not good or wise in the sense in which we normally understand these terms. If he were good and wise in the same sense that human beings can be, he would never have allowed the Pope to excommunicate Queen Elizabeth I, automatically putting English Catholics in an impossible position by making them enemies of the Crown. He would never have allowed the appalling famine in nineteeth-century Ireland, or in twentieth-century Ethiopia. But we do not think with God's mind, or feel with God's heart, or see with God's eyes. We cannot fathom his final purposes or ends. We cannot see how things look from the standpoint of eternity. 'My ways are not your ways', he said to the prophet, 'and my thoughts are not your thoughts.' If we really could see with God's eyes, then his justice, mercy and compassion would be evident. As it is, we have to accept that justice, in God, is so different from what we expect it to be, that it may often not appear to us like justice at all. We should expect this; our faith and general spiritual life will be securer for it.

To think with God's mind, to 'have the mind of Christ', as St Paul calls it, is not a thing we can achieve overnight. We have to grow into it gradually. Meanwhile, 'God is not wise; I am wiser than He is', because to my limited human wisdom, the infinite wisdom of God looks like mere folly.

Eckhart is very radical in the extent to which he wants us to be prepared to drop incomplete notions of God, however sanctified or traditional. He wants us to be prepared, when we are ready, to stop thinking of God as a 'Spirit' or as a 'Person' or as 'Father, Son and Holy Spirit'. There is a great deal of truth in these images; they are hallowed by the Church, and are, indeed, part of God's own revelation of himself. Therefore they are to be respected and used as the Church commands; but not to be rested in, not to be considered as final, for though they are true images, the mere fact of their being images at all means that they contain an element of limitation and illusion. So when the Eye of the Heart opens, and the spiritual intellect takes flight towards the Transcendent God, all these images have to go. Eckhart will not let us keep a single one of them. Not only is God not wise or good, but he is not a Person either, not Trinity, not Father, Son or Holy Spirit. In the end, he is not even God, for Eckhart makes the prayer: 'Therefore I pray God, that He may rid me of God.'

Even to say 'God' implies projection and externalization, and as long as we keep it up, we are not seeing the Reality unmediated, we have not reached the point when there is no more 'God' and 'I' but only Oneness.

It is high time we let Eckhart speak for himself, and describe in his own way the flight of spiritual intellect to its Transcendent God, beyond all names and forms. This is how he puts it in a German sermon:

Therefore, I say, if a man turns away from self and from created things, then – to the extent that you do this – you will attain oneness and blessedness in your soul's spark, which time and place never touched. This spark is opposed to all creatures; it wants nothing but God naked, just as He is. It is not satisfied with the Father, or the Son, or the Holy Ghost, or all three Persons so far as they preserve their several properties. I declare in truth, this light would not be satisfied with the unity of the whole fertility of the divine nature. In fact I will say still more, which sounds even stranger: I declare in all truth, by the eternal and everlasting truth, that this light is not content with the simple, changeless divine being which neither gives nor takes: rather it seeks to know whence this being comes, it wants to get into its simple Ground, into the Silent Desert, into which no distinction ever peeped of Father, Son or Holy Ghost.[1]

This, then, is the goal of our quest: the ultimate Reality, to which we can give no name, which we cannot describe in any image, to which we can ascribe no quality or distinction. We can unite with it and understand it only in darkness and silence, in a kind of unknowing knowing. Yet Eckhart himself uses images to evoke this imageless reality: he calls it the Source, the Root, the Ground, the Silent Desert. This is the desert spoken of by the prophet when he said: 'I will lead my bride into the desert, and speak to her heart' (Ho 2:14).

Plunging into the abyss of divinity, vanishing into the heart of the Silent Desert, is not something we do only when we are engaged in solitary meditation, in imageless prayer. The abyss, the desert, does not lie merely at the heart of our devotional and religious life; it lies at the heart of our whole life, and especially of our inner life, of that which goes on, often without our being fully aware of it, in the depths of ourselves. Every time we detach from an old, limited love, and open up to a newer, deeper, more universal one, we are taking a step nearer to our goal. It could also be that many people who seem to have rejected religion, who profess scepticism and unbelief, are really treading this same path without knowing it. What they are rejecting is not God, but the limited images of God which can actually, at a certain stage in life, hinder our perception of reality. What they are smashing is not God, but an idol, and their anger is a sacred anger. Once

1. Walshe, vol. 2, p. 105.

again we find ourselves in the world of the poets, for it is Yeats who gives clearest witness to this iconoclastic wrath in search of the transcendent:

> Then my delivered soul herself shall learn
> A darker knowledge and in hatred turn
> From every thought of God mankind has had.
> Thought is a garment and the soul's a bride
> That cannot in that trash and tinsel hide:
> Hatred of God may bring the soul to God.[2]

A fitting note on which to end this chapter.

2. *Supernatural Songs*, v.

4 Melting

'Deep calls unto deep' sang the Psalmist, uttering a truth
which is very relevant to our present concerns. For we are
faced now with two kinds of 'depth', different but closely
related. One is the depth of God, the Divine Abyss, the Silent
Desert, the 'God beyond God'. The other is the depth within
the human Self, which Eckhart calls the Ground, the Citadel,
Jerusalem, the Bride. This second depth is scarcely less
mysterious and awesome than the first; indeed it is its mirror-
image, reflecting it so faithfully that at times it is almost
impossible to distinguish between them. Eckhart, to the
dismay of his judges, did not always bother to make the
distinction clear. That is because for most of the time he is
not talking as a dogmatic theologian, but as a spiritual guide,
pointing out to us the road to union with God. Oneness, not
distinction, is his concern. What matters to him is not what
separates or distinguishes us from God, but what in us is
most like God, and above all, in what sense that 'likeness'
can be heightened and transcended until it becomes Unity.

How is it that we are able to become one with God? First,
because God himself desires it and calls us to it, giving us
the grace through the Incarnation, Death and Resurrection
of Christ. But there is also another reason. For two things to
love each other, and to be drawn to union with each other,
there must already be some kind of kinship or affinity between
them. This is axiomatic in Eckhart's thought. So if the soul
is destined for union with God, that must mean that it already
has within itself some element of affinity with God, something
which is already 'like' him. The conviction that this affinity
exists is not an invention of Eckhart's. It is declared openly
in the Book of Genesis, where God says: 'Let us make man
in our image and likeness.' What is it in us that most

resembles God, that in us which is his 'image' and 'likeness', which constitutes the *ground* on which our union with him becomes possible?

Theologians down the centuries have given many answers to this question. For example, it has been traditional, since St Augustine, to declare that we are 'Godlike' because we are rational beings, destined for immortality, and having within our immortal core a 'triumvirate' of powers – memory, understanding and will – which is the mirror-image of the Three Persons within the Trinity: Father, Son and Holy Spirit. Eckhart is entirely familiar with this teaching and makes frequent allusions to it. But he also sees that our kinship with God has a deeper basis than this. God is indeed a Trinity of Persons, but he is also a single, divine nature, an abyss of mystery beyond names, forms or distinctions, a 'silent desert'. If we are drawn to this abyss, this desert, this 'God beyond God', that must be because there is something in us which corresponds to it, which resembles it. Just as there is a 'Ground of Godhead', a 'God beyond God', so there is also in me a 'Ground of the Soul', a 'Me beyond Me'. The nameless depth in me cries out to the nameless depth in God: 'Deep calls unto deep.'

We have seen already that Eckhart's spiritual way is a way of paradox, of antithesis. Two apparently opposed realities will be brought by him into clashing confrontation, until the dualism separating them is transcended and their underlying unity emerges like sunlight after rain. We spent most of the preceding chapter gazing at a God who is utterly transcendent, utterly 'other', unlike anything we are accustomed to name or experience. Now we have to face the opposite, seemingly contradictory truth, that this 'transcendent other' has its analogue within ourselves – and even, from a certain point of view, can be said to be not different from ourselves.

If there really is this transcendent abyss within ourselves, then clearly we ought to become aware of it. Without it, how can our spiritual life ever get beyond the relatively superficial and external level? And even our personal relationships and activities in the world are going to be profoundly affected by the discovery of this 'Ground of the Soul'. It affects our whole notion of what it means to be a *person*, what it means to be *human*.

The Ground of the Soul, the True Image of God in Man, is a constant theme in Eckhart's writings. On almost every page it is there, either explicit or implicit. We shall look now at one of the places, in a German sermon, where he talks about it most clearly:

> I have sometimes said that there is a power in the soul which alone is free. Sometimes I have called it the guardian of the spirit, sometimes I have called it the light of the spirit, sometimes I have said that it is a little spark. But now I say that it is neither *this* nor *that*; and yet it is a *something* that is more exalted over 'this' and 'that' than are the heavens above the earth. So now I shall name it in nobler fashion than ever I did before, and yet it disowns the nobler name and mode, for it transcends them. It is free of all names and void of all forms, entirely exempt and free, as God is exempt and free in Himself. It is as completely one and simple as God is one and simple, so that no man can in any way glimpse it.[1]

When we read this passage, one of the most startling things we immediately notice about it is that it is applying to us, or at any rate to this mysterious 'ground' which we have within us, exactly the same language we have been applying previously to the Transcendent Abyss of Godhead. 'God is neither this nor that,' says Eckhart frequently, and now he says it of the Soul's Ground. It transcends the created order, just as the heavens are more exalted than the earth. It is 'exempt' and 'free'. This is not the place to go into the question of 'exemption' and 'freedom' which needs fuller inquiry later on. But we cannot afford to pass over the question of how I, a finite, limited created human being, can have something within me which is 'neither this nor that', which in some sense transcends the created order. In particular we cannot afford to pass over the question of how it can be 'free of all names and forms'. Have we not been saying that to 'strip away names and forms' means to withdraw our projections, our illusory and limited imagery, so as to touch on the naked reality of God? Is there then a naked reality of *ourselves*, too, normally disguised by projections, which we need to strip away if we are to get at the truth?

Eckhart claims that there is. 'I' am not who I think I am,

1. Walshe, vol. 1, p. 76.

and 'You' are not who you think you are. What we call 'I' and 'You' is indeed a projection, and if we go far enough in withdrawing the projections and in piercing the veils, we shall reach a point at which there is no longer any 'I' or 'You'. We shall also reach a point, much sooner, at which we shall come to realize that our true 'self' has nothing whatever to do with *function*. I am not any of the things I do, and I am not any of the roles I assume, either in the face of my fellow-humans, or when alone by myself.

This flies right in the face of what our modern life encourages us to think about ourselves; for we are accustomed to see ourselves almost totally in terms of function. We identify ourselves with what we do, with the role we believe we are called upon to play in society. 'What are *you*?' we are asked, and we answer: a lawyer, a chimney-sweep, a doctor, a dustman, a priest. Yet these are only functions, things we do; they are not *us*. Eckhart is emphatic that our truest self, in the core of our being, has nothing to do with function and nothing to do with roles which we may assume, either for our own benefit or for others. 'It is as if you were to name someone a carpenter; you are not calling him "soul" or "man" or "Henry" or anything according to his own proper being; you are naming him only according to his proper work or function.'[2]

These roles and functions are real projections, like the ones we foist onto God, and we apply them to ourselves for exactly the same reason: because they give us a sense of security, a sense of identity and belonging. They prevent us from glimpsing the awful void and emptiness within ourselves: they make us feel solid, needed, valued and permanent. And indeed, like our 'God projections', they may not be entirely illusory. I may really have a natural aptitude for gardening, or music, or finance, which can be put to good use in society and thus give me a name and a sort of identity. But it is not my real name or my real identity. My real 'self' is something quite other and is as much concealed as revealed by these social roles. And sometimes unforeseen circumstances can occur which shatter them and display their hollowness: the woman, whom her husband has always believed to be a

2. Author's translation; cf. Walshe, vol. 1, p. 171.

faithful and contented wife, suddenly walks out, leaving a
note on the mantelpiece; the clergyman, who has always
been considered a perfect model of decorum, suddenly shocks
everyone with an indelicate joke at a garden party. 'Role-
gaps', or the incompatibility between the external social role
and the inner personality, are considered as a problem in
society. But Eckhart would not consider them necessarily a
problem; rather, he would see them as a possible sign of hope.
By exposing the illusory nature of the role, the true self might
be enabled to surface. By shattering the shell, there is a
chance that we might get at the kernel.

But it is not only our external, social personalities which
are a tissue of projections and illusions. The same is true of
much of our inner, private world, of what we may well be
tempted to regard as our real 'self', but in fact is not. We are
not our social functions or roles; but neither are we our private
emotions or thoughts. This becomes clear to anyone who
makes a serious practice of sitting still in meditation. The
kind of meditation I am talking about here is not meditation
upon anything or *about* anything; it consists simply of sitting
still for a lengthy period and simply *watching* the various
thoughts and emotions which arise in the mind; not trying to
resist them, drive them out, or change them, but simply
watching them without identifying with them or being
engulfed by them. This is not, strictly speaking, a religious
exercise; it is not prayer, and it has nothing to do with God;
in fact it is possible to practise it without believing in God at
all. Nevertheless it is an extremely useful exercise; so much
so that certain Buddhist schools make it their basic spiritual
practice. Why? Because if we watch our emotions and
thoughts for long enough, we may eventually become aware
of something within us which is *not* these emotions or
thoughts. If I am watching something, then I must be
different and distinct from what I am watching. The fact that
I am able to watch my thoughts means that they are different
from me; I am not them. I am, indeed, none of those things
which I am accustomed to regard as 'myself'; I am not my
body, nor my mind, nor my emotions, nor am I all these
things taken together. So what am I? What is 'me'?

There is something within me which is at all times perfectly
detached, tranquil and serene. It is never excited about

anything, never downcast or depressed by anything. It is like
a deep, perhaps even bottomless, lake; my various thoughts
and emotions are like ripples or waves upon the surface.
But below the surface, in the depths, there are no ripples;
everything is still. Strange fish live there, and feathery fronds
of aquatic plants. Once the turbulence on the surface has
died down and the water becomes quite clear, we can see into
the depths and become aware of what lives there. But even
this is not the lake itself; it is not me. 'I' am that which
contains it all, the water which is still water, whether it is
calm or ruffled, fresh or salt, thronged with fish or totally
empty. This is the true, the permanent self, which we may
become aware of once we detach from our various projections
and activities which are not *us* but only things we do and
functions we perform.

Unless we become aware of the Permanent Self, we shall
be tyrannized continually by our thoughts and emotions. How
can we avoid it, since we have no place of refuge from them;
indeed, we think we *are* them? This creates disunity and
fragmentation in our lives; because we are a different 'self'
depending on the moods or activities of the moment. I am
one person when eating; another when walking; another when
at work; yet another when talking to my wife. There is nothing
to give any unity or continuity to my identity, nothing to give
it coherence or to hold it together. I am not one self but a
sequence of different or even conflicting selves. Eckhart calls
this being lost in 'multiplicity' and in 'alien images'. It is a
state of unawareness of who we really are. We are entirely
conditioned and determined by influences from outside, which
means that we are not really able to 'do' anything at all,
because there is no 'self' in us to do anything. What we believe
to be our 'action' is just reaction, robot-like and automatic, to
external stimuli and conditioning. Action, in the true sense,
is only possible for one who has penetrated to the true Self,
the Ground of the Soul, and has learned to act from that
centre. We are not real, unified 'selves', we are not capable
of true action, until we learn to enter that Ground. Genuine
action is never determined from without, but arises spon-
taneously and freely from within.

It is easy to see from all this that the Ground of the Soul
has a very high degree of detachment from the everyday

world, and from what we normally regard as our 'identity'
and our 'life'. It is exalted above them, says Eckhart, as the
heavens are exalted above the earth. Nothing earthy can
really touch it. It transcends space and time. Anyone who
enters the soul's Ground, no longer cares about the past or
the future: he is aware only of the present moment, and the
present moment is shot through with Divine Light, because
it is in the present, and in the present alone, that the world
of time touches the world of eternity. Standing within this
impregnable citadel, we are troubled neither by the thought
of our past experiences nor of possible troubles and preoccupations still to come; we are totally purified, rinsed and
cleansed, and we stand upright on the borders of the world
of time, gazing into eternity.

Many people reading this book will be wondering by now
how they are expected to get into this Ground, which seems
such a lofty and sublime reality and which they may not find
many signs of in their own personal life. A fuller discussion
of this question will be reserved for a later chapter, but at
least something needs to be said about it now. And here we
come up against a typically Eckhartian paradox, of the kind
which characterizes his spiritual Way. The Ground of the
Soul is, as we have seen, the true Self. But we cannot get
inside it, learn to live in it and act from within it, unless we
strip away what we normally regard as our 'self'. We must
throw away self in order to find Self. It is obvious why this
has to be so. Most of our life consists of a tissue of projections
and false identifications, whereby we imagine that we *are* our
thoughts, feelings, actions and roles in the world. We have to
let go of all that. We have to learn not to do, not to be
anything, but simply to *be*. The moment we set ourselves
some sort of goal or ambition, then we are trapped by another
limited, illusory image, another false 'self'. The Ground of
the Soul has no ambitions or goals; not even the goal of
knowing itself. It is simply free, restful, open and receptive
to the reality of the present moment, and whatever there is
of God in it. This detached openness and receptivity, this
refusal to *aim* at anything, is one of its most Godlike
characteristics.

Eckhart is fond of saying that in God there is no 'why',
which means that he acts without goals or ambitions. What

purpose did he have in creating heaven and earth? None
whatever. He gained nothing by it; he possesses every perfection within himself, he needs no one else. He needs nothing
outside himself. The purpose of creation was simply to create,
it was not *for* anything. It was like a game or a play; he did
it simply because it was 'fun' to do. The Ground of the Soul
mirrors this quality in him. It is free from goals and purposes,
it has no 'why'. Therefore, the moment we are governed by
some goal or purpose, we are not within the Ground but
outside, in the world of the false, not the true, Self. In many
ways, the best image of God creating the world, and the holy
man acting from within his own Ground, is not a master-
architect planning a cathedral, or a master-engineer building
a suspension bridge, but a child playing with a spinning top.

So if we knit our brows together in ferocious concentration,
and sit for long hours in meditation, thinking that we shall
thereby enter the Ground of the Soul, we are sadly mistaken.
There is no surer way to miss the mark than this. Why?
Because if I say to myself: 'I am now going to enter the
Ground of my Soul, even if it kills me to do it', then I have
set myself a goal, and it is the nature of the Ground to be
free from goals. We cannot enter it by resolving to enter it.
We enter it by not trying to enter it, by not thinking about
it or aiming at it, by being simply relaxed, free, spontaneous,
untroubled, open to the present moment and whatever it
contains. The more deeply and totally we are able to do this,
the more deeply we shall be entering the Soul's Ground. It
is true that certain activities are more conducive to this state
of mind than others. It is easier to do it when sitting in
meditation than when acting as a barman or as a waiter in
a restaurant. But, strictly speaking, it should be possible to
perform *all* activities in this frame of mind, and this is
precisely what happens in the case of the person who has
learned to live more or less permanently within his own
Ground. Meditation may be useful as a start, but we should
aim at applying the state of mind learned in meditation to
all the activities of our life.

It is this Ground, says Eckhart, which is the truest and
deepest Image of God in Man, for it is the analogue of the
Abyss of Godhead, the Silent Desert, the Nameless Transcendent. It is that in us which has most affinity with God. God,

in the truest sense, has no name; he is not the God we imagine
and address in our prayers. Similarly the Ground of the Soul
has no name; it is not any of those things that other people
recognize us by; it is not even any of those things whereby
we normally recognize ourselves. It is transcendent and nameless, like God himself; therefore Eckhart says: 'God, who is
nameless, is ineffable: He has no name. In the Ground, it
[the soul] is as ineffable as He is.'[3]

Being that in us which is most like God, it is also that in
which union with God takes place. It is the inner sanctuary
where we and God meet and become one.

Plunging into the Transcendent Abyss of Godhead, and
sinking into the Nameless Ground of our own Soul, are really
one and the same process. The journey into the depths of
God, and the journey into the depths of ourselves, are not
really different. Theologically and metaphysically it may be
possible to distinguish them, but on the level of experience
and action they are one. Eckhart is emphatic that God cannot
be found or grasped in the external world, but only in the
inner world. If we seek him outside, we shall find him
nowhere; if we seek him within, we shall find him everywhere.
This is not to say that only the inner world is real. Both are
real; both have their own measure of importance. But it
is the inner world which has the priority and the greater
importance. The inner contains the outer, while transcending
it. Having discovered God within, we can then discover him
without; but never the other way round.

That which is most inward and secret in God is the
Godhead, the Abyss. That which is most inward and secret
in us is the Ground of the Soul. When these two inward,
secret depths meet and unite, then we are one with God. This
clearly necessitates detachment from externals, withdrawal
and concentration of energy within. The two 'depths', in God
and in us, are inviolate, closed, remote worlds, in which there
is no name, no image, no activity, but only stillness and
oneness.

But here again we stumble upon the essentially paradoxical
character of the spiritual way. Having discovered stillness
and oneness in God and in ourselves, we cannot rest there.

3. Author's translation; cf. Walshe, vol. 1. p. 172.

The Transcendent Ground, in God and in the soul, may be the fundamental and truest reality; but it is not the whole of reality, and only the whole of reality will satisfy the spiritual intellect. God does not remain forever locked within his impregnable fortress of Transcendence, nor does the Ground of the Soul remain forever closed to the outward world. God speaks himself forth, in the Persons of the Trinity, and in the Creation. We also 'speak ourselves forth', in a manner we shall go into more closely later. This return to the outer world is described by Eckhart in a number of ways: as a 'going out', a 'speaking forth', a 'boiling', or even a 'boiling over'; and lastly, as in the title of this chapter, a 'melting', (in German, *uss-schmelzen;* in Latin *liquescens*). The inviolate, pure, crystalline world of transcendent oneness melts and flows out of itself. This melting and outflowing is the mystery of what it means to be a *Person.* If we want to understand what a Person is – either divine or human – it is in the process of *melting* that we find the answer.

Now we find ourselves faced with one of the deepest and most perplexing mysteries in Christianity: that of the Trinity. Yet we should not call it a 'mystery' in the sense of something totally incomprehensible and closed to us, but in the sense of a *depth* which is to be plumbed gradually throughout the whole of life, through experience as much as by thinking and talking. Indeed, the etymology of the word 'mystery' – meaning 'that which is not to be talked about' – shows that it is experience, rather than speech, which leads us into these depths. Yet we are not, today, accustomed to see the Trinity as having any relevance or bearing on our own personal lives. It has become merely a theological puzzle, a metaphysical conundrum, a logical absurdity, a piece of insane mathematics which refuses to work out. Eckhart, however, places it right at the heart of our spiritual life as we actually live it. He does not do this by inviting us to 'contemplate' it, or to make it an object of devotion, something outside and separate from ourselves. Rather, he invites us to be caught up into the inner life of the Trinity, to actually participate in that unutterable communion and union of the Three, in the silence of eternity. In fact, to the extent that we are true human beings, true *persons*, we are already participating in that secret life, however imperfectly or unconsciously. Conversely, the deeper and more consciously we participate in it, the more *human* and the more *personal* we become.

So we shall look now at this mystery of personhood, of 'melting out' which gives this chapter its name.

God is utterly transcendent; so much we have seen already. We cannot hope to understand or unite with him until we penetrate the core of his transcendence, which is above all names, forms, images and activities. Yet neither can we shut him up or imprison him in his Silent Desert. He refuses to be imprisoned or shut up, even in his own transcendence! It is true that if we try to enclose him in images and projections, he affirms that he is above and beyond all that. But if we try to insist that he is *only* transcendence, then he catches us out again by emerging from his secret citadel and affirming himself on the outside. He is so transcendent that he transcends even his own transcendence. Here we are at the very heart of the Way of Paradox. If we seek God without, he retreats within; if we seek him within, he affirms himself without. It is only by yielding to this giddy metaphysical switchback that we can come to grasp the full reality of God. And it is within the Trinity that the whole paradox of 'inner' and 'outer' starts. If we grasp it there, we shall be able to grasp it throughout the whole of life.

God, then, does not remain locked in his inviolate Transcendence. He has to pour himself out; the crystal has to melt. He has to give utterance or expression to the infinite secret hidden within his own depths. Being of infinite power, his utterance and expression of himself is perfect and totally adequate to the Reality which it utters. It is not at all like when *we* utter something or try to give expression to what we know or feel; for our outward expression is never fully adequate to the reality of what we are trying to express; for us, however eloquent and sincere we may be, there will always remain some residue of truth which cannot be expressed – even to ourselves – and therefore has to remain unspoken. But when God speaks out of the depths of his mystery, there can be no such inadequacy; in uttering himself, he utters himself *totally*, and there is no residue of mystery left which remains unuttered. Here we plunge into the thick of the paradox. He expresses himself so totally and so adequately that the expression and the truth expressed are not two

different realities but one reality. God puts himself so totally
into his expression of himself that it *is* himself. It is not
different from him, there are not two Gods, one uttering and
the other being uttered, but the Speaker and the Spoken are
one and the same God. God as Speaker is called Father,
because 'Father' denotes origin. God as Spoken is called Son,
because 'Son' denotes someone generated or originated. We
might sum all this up by saying that Father and Son are
simply God expressing himself to himself. The Father
expresses the whole of his reality in the Son, and the Son
reflects that back with total truthfulness, so that God is not
divided or diminished by his self-expression, but remains one
and undivided within himself.

As Eckhart says in several sermons, to go out and yet
remain within is a great mystery and wonder. If it is a great
thing for God to express himself totally, and for his expression
to reflect him totally, it is an equally great thing that
Expressor and Expressed should remain one single being,
whole and undivided, still enclosed within itself. Therefore
this unity, this non-division between Speaker and Spoken,
becomes also a Divine Person making up the triad: it is the
Holy Spirit, who is called the bond between the Father and
the Son. If Father and Son are the mystery of the *oneness*
between speaker and speech, the Spirit is the mystery which
ensures that they do not become two Gods, but remain one
God.

This formula of Eckhart's 'going out and yet remaining
within' is the key to all spiritual life. Going out, yet remaining within, is also what happens in the creating and sustain-
ing of the whole universe. The same mystery, as we shall see
later, is enacted in the Ground of the Soul when it is united
with God. It is enacted further when the truly spiritual and
awakened man turns towards the world to perform works of
compassion in it. Now we can see how it is that the Trinity
is not some pale, bloodless abstraction, dreamed up by philosophers and theologians. On the contrary, it lies right at the
heart of life; indeed, we only truly *live* to the extent that we
are caught up in it and share in it. We shall see later how
the mystery of going out yet remaining within operates in
creation, in mystical union, and in enlightened activity in the
world. For the moment we should notice just two points about

it which will help us to see its importance for us in helping us to understand ourselves, God, and the world we live in.

First of all, the Trinity is above all a mystery of *power*. This is not something which is always immediately apparent when theologians talk about it, or even when icon-painters try to depict it. It can seem a very tranquil, aloof and static affair. But the truth cannot possibly be like that, since the true God is a God of power. The truth is dynamic. For God to utter himself in the Son is an act of tremendous power; indeed, infinite power. For that utterance to remain within, and not 'spill over' on the outside, producing a second God, is also a work of infinite power. To be Three yet One, Spoken yet Unspoken, is a paradox, and paradox implies tension. When we say 'tension', again we are talking the language of power, for tension generates energy. The language which Eckhart uses to describe how the Three Persons arise and interrelate is all power-language. They 'melt' out of each other, into each other, and into the one Divine Nature which they all share, from which they all emerge and into which they all return. Eckhart does not speak only of 'melting' but also of 'glowing' and 'boiling'. All of this suggests a colossal accumulation of energy, yet all held in total balance and control. This again is a secret to be found throughout the universe, including our own lives. When *we* act, and pour ourselves out in the world and in relationships with other people, this involves loss of energy, dissipation. But to learn to pour out while remaining inwardly detached, to be at once in movement yet also in repose, is largely what the spiritual life is all about: to the extent that we have learned that we are true Persons, true images of God, true sharers in the swirling, glowing, energic life of the Trinity. To live like that also means to be untiring, for it brings about accumulation, not loss, of energy. Power is always greatest when it is accompanied by the greatest restraint. Here again, Eckhart's teaching is one which makes perfect sense to Far Eastern adepts, of Taoism or Zen. Yet at the same time it could not be more Christian, for it is grounded on the Trinity – the central mystery of the Christian faith. We may indeed, if we wish, speak of this inner life of the Trinity as one of 'peace', 'tranquillity' and 'contemplation', provided we do not take these terms to imply inertia or lack of energy. On the contrary they imply maximum generation of energy, held in maximum equilibrium, or rather, infinite generation of energy in infinite equilibrium.

Thus, to be a Person means to be initiated into the mystery of true power.

The second thing we must understand about Persons, in God, and also, by extension, in ourselves, is that they tend essentially to transcend themselves, go out of themselves, and seek union. It is traditional, and correct, in theology, to see the Persons within the Trinity as *relations*; and by extension we can say that to be a Person, whether Divine or human, means to *relate*. But this way of looking at it will lead us astray unless we recognize that the Trinitarian Persons are not content with merely *relating*; they want to *unite*. Father, Son and Holy Spirit do not merely commune; they become one. They melt out of the Silent Desert, the Abyss of Godhead, they melt into each other, and they melt back into the Abyss. We have to talk about this 'melting out' and 'melting back' as if they occurred successively, one after the other; but in fact they are simultaneous and prolonged throughout eternity. The Silent Desert cannot remain enclosed and dark; out of it the Persons of Father, Son and Holy Spirit emerge. Yet they, for their part, cannot remain distinct, but commune, unite and return to the transcendent Oneness of the Silent Desert. This, too, is what it means to be a Person – to aim perpetually at transcendence, oneness emerging into multiplicity, multiplicity returning to oneness. The implications of all this for our own lives, for our relations with other people, with the Church, with society and with the world, are far-reaching. I shall be trying to spell out some of these implications in the chapters which follow.

To be a Person, then, means to have learned the secret and paradoxical art: to go out, yet remain within; to exert power, yet exercise restraint; to transcend, yet remain oneself; to be in movement, yet be in total repose. This is a deeper concept of personhood than is to be found in most thinkers, either ancient or modern. But it is the truest, being based on the reality of God and of the Human Self.

If we wish to penetrate this mystery, what must we do? We must first enter the formless Abyss, both in God and in the depths of ourselves, in the soul's Ground. From that we emerge reborn into the life of communion represented by the

Trinity. But what is it that can lead us into the Abyss, and into the secret communion and union of the Three? This is the Divine Word, the Son, who took human form as Jesus of Nazareth. This Word, in whom the universe was created, and in whom we are reborn into God, is the subject of the next chapter.

5 The Voice of God

In us, as in God, there is a nameless abyss. In us, as in God, there is a flowing-out into relations, into a world of Persons and Names. In us, as in God, there is a dissatisfaction with simply 'relating' and 'communing'; there is an insatiable and insistent desire to return to oneness.

The stage is thus set for our union with God. We are mirror-images of him; we have within us something which corresponds to the transcendent Godhead, and also something which corresponds to the personal God, flowing out into Father, Son and Spirit who interrelate and unite. Like attracts like, so God and we are destined for union. One depth calls out to the other. Yet the fact remains that there is a vast gulf between us and God. He is Creator, we are created; there can be no greater difference and separateness than that. How is that gulf to be bridged? On the one hand there is infinite energy, fiery, swirling, melting and boiling in total equilibrium which holds all together in total unity; on the other hand we have our drab, petty, everyday lives in the kitchen, the office and the workshop. Who or what can span the gulf and effect a marriage between two worlds so utterly different?

This is the work of the Creative Word. This Word is first uttered within the Trinity, as God the Son, in the eternal silence of heaven. But it is also uttered 'outside', bringing the created universe into being, giving it shape, order, direction. Finally it is uttered in the human world, taking flesh as Jesus, the carpenter of Nazareth. It is thus like a keynote whose vibrations are felt in every part of the universe, linking all together. 'In the beginning', says the evangelist, 'was the Word.' But in saying that, he is implying that the Word is not only in the beginning, but also in the end, and in everything which lies between. Whether we know it or not, we are vibrating in harmony with it now, at this very moment. If we did not do so, we would immediately cease to exist, because it is only by virtue of our 'tuning' to that note that we have life and being at all.

It is through this Word that we are united with God. Through the Word, the depths of God are spoken out into our world; through that same Word, we and our world are spoken back into the depths of God.

No mystery was ever more universally known than this – nor more universally misunderstood. This proclamation of the evangelist – 'In the beginning was the Word' – would, if we could only hear it, shake us to the core of our being. But we do not hear it. We are unable to hear it, because we have forgotten what a 'Word' is. A 'Word' is three things. First, it is a *communication*, it tells us something. Second, it speaks the *truth*, it tells us about something *real*. Finally, it arises from the depths of the speaker, which means that it arises out of *silence*. There can be no Word without a Silence from which it emerges, which it expresses and to which it returns. It is precisely this Silence, this Depth which makes it 'true' and able to communicate.

It is perhaps this last element, of silence and depth, which is most important, which distinguishes a true 'Word' from a false one. Most of the words we use today, in everyday speech, are false. They do not arise out of anything really deep in ourselves, and they lack truth, being often designed to hide or distort reality rather than reveal it. Such are the words used by politicians, commercial advertisers, and even, some-times, by preachers and theologians – by all, in fact, who feel obliged to get something said rather than to have something to say. Much of our everyday conversation is the same – mere tittle-tattle, expressing nothing really deep or true, but aiming simply at 'filling the gap'. Filling what gap? The gap of silence. Silence is one of the most dreaded realities in a world of empty, false words, because silence leads us into the depths of ourselves. Yet no word, however eloquent it may seem, can have real depth, truth, or power to communicate, unless it arises from silence – unless it *expresses*, rather than obliterates that silence.

This is a truth which we can verify for ourselves in our own lives. If two people know each other very well, and are, on a deep, intuitive level, 'in tune' with each other, they do not feel any necessity to be continually talking. Often, in their conversation, it is what is unsaid, rather than what is said, which counts. That is the element of depth and silence, which is indispensable to real rapport and communication. In these circumstances, words are few, but telling and to the point. They arise out of the depths, and they express silence rather than obliterate it.

The same principle is at work in the best music. For this, also, is an important fact, too often overlooked, that music, at its most genuine, is not merely background noise, more or less pleasing, but is a *language*. Just as much as spoken and written language, music *expresses* things: thoughts, feelings, reactions, a whole vision of life and of the world we live in. It is, therefore, just as much a 'Word' as anything spoken or written in a book. It also has the same relation to silence. There is some music which aims at shattering and obliterating silence. There is another kind of music which does not shatter silence, but seems rather to be an extension and expression of it. It is this second kind which is the true music, because it is the most truthful – it arises from the depths, from that in us which is most genuine. In this it resembles the sounds of nature – largely banished from our modern, mechanized world – for it is also characteristic of natural sounds that they seem to heighten rather than destroy silence. Anyone who listens to wind stirring the leaves of trees, to waves breaking on the sand, even to thunder splitting the sky, will have no difficulty in grasping this. It is not simply that silence precedes and follows these sounds; it remains as a background to them, and even expresses itself in them. They, in their turn, point back to it. We cannot claim, therefore, not to know what a true 'word' is. It is something we come across frequently in our own experience, and all the more frequently if our lives are lived at a genuine, deep level. If we can listen to the silence behind the wind stirring the grass, behind the greatest music, and behind the deepest conversation which we have with others, then we have some notion, however faint, of the Supreme Word spoken by the Father out of the silent depths of the Abyss. All words are echoes of that Word. To a nervous person on a winter's night, it might seem a mere poetic metaphor to say that the howling wind is an echo of the voice of God. But it is not mere metaphor; it is the truth.

So now, faithful to the Way of Antithesis and Paradox, we can swing back from our human world into the Divine World of the Trinity. Guided by what we know of true 'words' in our own experience, we may hope to grasp something of that Word which is in the beginning with God, in which God speaks himself forth and brings the whole universe into being.

Eckhart draws a distinction between 'God' and 'Godhead'. What he calls 'Godhead' is the Silent Desert, the Abyss of Transcendence, above all names or forms, which does not beget, does not create, and is not a 'Person'. What he calls 'God' is that which is Personal, which utters itself forth and expresses itself, and thus receives names: Father, Son and Holy Spirit, all summed up and expressed in the single word 'God'. The Godhead is silent and unuttered, it has no name; when it utters itself, it becomes 'Father'; the utterance itself is Son; yet the two are totally one, both in each other and in the silent Abyss of Godhead from which they emerge and to which they return; this total oneness and unity is itself a Person, and is called 'Holy Spirit'. In some ways this 'Spirit' is the deepest mystery of all, for it shows how that which comes out is still enclosed within; that which is spoken is still silent; that which is distinct is still one. The three Persons must be one, because there is nothing intervening to separate them; they relate directly, im-mediately, 'without mediation'. Eckhart explains this, in his typically lighthearted way, as follows:

> A master says, if all mediation were gone between me and this wall, I would be *on* the wall, but not *in* the wall. It is not thus in spiritual matters, for the one is always in the other: that which embraces is that which is embraced, for it embraces nothing but itself.[1]

He then goes on to remark 'This is subtle', and adds, with characteristic humour: 'He who understands it has been preached to enough.' With that we can only agree.

But if from a certain point of view the Spirit is the deepest mystery, since he is the principle of unity in distinction, silence in utterance, we may also, from a different point of

1. Walshe, vol. 1, p. 121.

view, regard the Son as the deepest mystery because he is the most *central*. Through the Son, the Godhead is uttered and becomes God the Father. Through the same Son, the universe is uttered and becomes Creation. The Son, again, is uttered in the world of men as the carpenter of Nazareth, Jesus, and thus becomes Redeemer. Thus the Son is central: in the Trinity, in the universe and in human life. He is what God, Creation and Mankind have in common; he is the linchpin of the universe. It is in him, as St Paul says, that 'all things are held together'. He is the foundation-stone of the edifice; the tonic of the musical scale; the hub of the cosmic wheel.

We have just said that the Son, the Word, is that which God, man and the universe have in common. We need to reflect on this a little and ponder its implications. When the list of allegedly 'heretical' statements was called from Eckhart's works and presented to the court, there was one especially which caught the judges' attention: 'At once, and as soon as God was, when He begot His co-eternal Son as God fully equal to Himself, He also created the world.'[2] This worried the judges because it seemed to imply that there is no difference between God uttering himself as the Son, within the Trinity, and God uttering himself outside the Trinity in the created universe. If this is what Eckhart means, it is pantheism, confusing God with the universe, saying that the universe is *begotten* from God in the same way that the Son is, saying that the universe *is* God the Son! Fortunately, Eckhart is saying no such thing, as becomes obvious when this statement is seen in the general context of his thought. He is saying that God utters himself in two ways: internally and silently, within the Trinity, externally and aloud in the creation of the universe. These two ways are, of course, from one point of view, very different. Within the Trinity God utters himself totally and expresses himself totally, so that the utterance is not different from himself; it, too, is God. The created universe, however, is not a total expression of the reality of God; it is only an image or reflection of it, very partial and imperfect. It is not the Word; it is only the echo of the Word. Yet it is the same Word which is being uttered in both cases. The speaking forth of the Son, within the

2. Walshe, vol. 1, p. xlvii.

Trinity, echoes and resounds in the creation of the universe. So from that point of view there are not two utterances, but only one. God, in speaking his Word within himself, also brings the universe into being. This is how Eckhart interprets the text of the Psalm which says 'God spoke once, but I heard him twice' (Ps 61:12). God speaks only once and speaks only one Word, but it is *heard* twice: within God, in the Trinity; and outside God, in creation.

> The prophet says, 'God spoke one, and I heard two'. That is true: God spoke but once. His utterance is but one. In His Word He speaks His Son and the Holy Ghost and all creatures, which are all one utterance in God. But the prophet says, 'I heard two', that is, I heard God and the creatures.[3]

In other words, creation is a kind of *echo* of the Word spoken in God. Within the Trinity, the Word is spoken, within the universe it echoes. But whether spoken or echoing, there is only one Word. So the Word really is that which God and the universe have in common.

It is therefore through the Word, and only through the Word, that we can achieve *unity* with ourselves, with other people, with the world around us, or with God. It is because we have lost touch with the Word, because we are not in tune with it, that our inner life is full of tension and contradiction, our relations with others full of fear and violence, our lives fragmented, disordered and without direction. To be at one with ourselves, with others, with the world, and with God, is only possible for one who is grounded and rooted in the Word.

What does that mean: to be grounded and rooted in the Word?

We saw earlier in this chapter that the Word echoes and resounds throughout the whole universe. Everything which exists at all vibrates in harmony with it. Therefore, it must also be resounding within us at every moment; especially since we have been created specifically for this purpose, to be a kind of 'echo-chamber' for it. That is why we have within us this nameless, transcendent depth which we call the Ground of the Soul; the Ground is a kind of hollow chamber, an empty, inner space, in which the Word can be spoken and echoed. To be united with God, to be one with God, is

3. Walshe, vol. 1, p. 148.

actually the same thing as having the Word spoken within us, so that our whole being vibrates with it, and becomes its sound-board. Some people reading Eckhart have found it perverse and peculiar that he likes to talk of the mystical union between man and God in the imagery of 'birth', of 'giving birth to the Son in the Ground of the Soul' or of having the Word 'spoken in the Ground of the Soul'. But there is nothing arbitrary about this way of talking; it is the most accurate way possible of describing what actually happens. The whole spiritual life is directed to this end. What is the purpose of all this detachment, renunciation, letting go, casting aside self-will, that Eckhart talks about perpetually? It is simple to create an empty, hollow space within ourselves, so that we can become a sound-board, or echo-chamber, for the Word.

Once this happens, we are drawn immediately into the inner life of the Trinity and even of the Transcendent Godhead. It is not simply that the Trinity suddenly 'occupies the centre' of our lives, that we 'enter into relations' with it, that it becomes 'meaningful' or 'relevant' to us. That would be altogether too superficial a way of describing the situation. Rather, it is that once we become rooted and grounded in the Word echoing within us, then, to the extent that we do this, we 'become' that Word, and *its life is our life*. We share in the relation of the Son to the Father; we are 'Sons' in the Son, enlivened and unified by the Holy Spirit, begotten by the Father, emerging from him and returning to him. We also share in the Transcendent Godhead, the Silent Desert, the 'ground' of communion between the Three Persons.

This is what the spiritual life, at its deepest, really means: not merely 'believing' in God, or even 'worshipping' God, but living and dwelling *in* God. We are no longer mere 'followers' of Christ, we live in Christ, sharing in his relationship to the Father, being 'sons' as he is Son, through the Holy Spirit. What this means for our inner spiritual life is something we must go into in more detail later in this book. For the moment we need to see how this living *in* Christ, in the Word, in the heart of the Trinity, is going to affect our attitude to the world around us, the world of people and things.

Let us suppose, then, that the spiritual intellect, the Eye

of the Heart, is open in us, and we are seeing God as clearly and immediately as is possible for us in this present life. That is to say, we are seeing the Father through the eyes of the Son, illuminated by the Holy Spirit. We are seeing God in God. This means that we are also able to see the *world* in God; to see the *world* as God sees it. That Eckhart should have thought it possible for mortal men, in this life, to see the world as God sees it, is very astonishing; but that he did think so is beyond question. Some years ago a book was written by C. F. Kelley, called *Meister Eckhart on Divine Knowledge*. This is a difficult book, taxing even for the professional theologian and the philosopher, and is therefore likely to remain unread save by a small circle of specialists and experts; which is a pity, since it contains an extremely important insight, without which much in Eckhart's writing must appear obscure or even nonsensical. What is this insight? Precisely this: that it is possible for human beings, living, thinking and acting in God, to think, see, and do, as God does. Instead of standing within the created world, looking in it for signs of a God who is outside it, we stand within God, and it is the world which now appears outside. When we stand within the world, God appears as totally transcendent and 'other'. When we stand within God, however, it is the world which appears as 'other', but not by any means transcendent; on the contrary, we are greater than it. It appears as a pale and imperfect reflection of the dazzling and brilliant Truth in which we are living and making our home. Is this the way Eckhart himself looked at the world? Kelley believes so; indeed, he maintains that practically *all* Eckhart's thinking is like this, not only when he is thinking about the created universe, but also when he is thinking about God and the Godhead, the Trinity, the Creation, Incarnation and Redemption; the whole Christian Revelation, in fact. This, in Kelley's view, is what makes Eckhart's thought so baffling for many people; it is because they are expecting him to think in the normal human way, approaching God from the outside, through the world, when in fact he is doing the exact opposite, standing within the heart of God and looking out.

It is perhaps open to question whether Eckhart *always* thinks and talks from this point of view. But that he *often* does is clear, perhaps more often than anyone before him or after

him. He does not lack predecessors: there are passages in St
Augustine which equal his in brilliance and depth. He does
not altogether lack followers, either: there are moments of
insight in Tauler, Nicholas of Cusa and St John of the Cross
which are very comparable to his own. But what is momentary and sporadic in them is frequent, and even usual, in
him. It is perhaps this particular perspective of his that we
have most to learn from. It puts, for example, the whole
question of the 'existence of God' on a totally different footing
from the one to which we are accustomed. To approach God
from the outside, through the world, is the path taken by St
Thomas Aquinas in his famous 'proofs' for God's existence
which get such a bad press today. Aquinas looks at the world
of change and deduces that there must be an Unchanging
Reality behind it; he looks at the evidence of order and mean-
ingfulness in the world, and deduces that there must be a
Designer and Planner behind it. In other words, the world
proves God. But Eckhart would find this view rather amusing.
For him, it is God who proves the world. God is the *prime
datum*, the given, unquestionable reality; everything else is
merely derived and deduced.

It would be easy for us to take fright at this point and
declare: 'This is no doubt very sublime and deep; but it is
totally foreign to my experience and utterly beyond my
capacity.' But is it? To have the Word spoken in the Ground
of the Soul, to give birth to the Son within the deepest core
of ourselves, to live in God and see with God's eyes – this is,
no doubt, a very awesome mystery; but we should not
conclude too hastily that it is necessarily beyond our reach.
We must understand that this is not a question of having
some kind of supernormal experience, of trance or of vision,
for example. Eckhart rarely talks about these experiences of
ecstasy; indeed, almost never. And it is clear that he had very
little interest in them and attached very little importance to
them. Prayer and meditation clearly have their value in life
and are not to be omitted; but they are not the whole of life.
The 'Birth of the Son', the 'Speaking of the Word in the
Ground of the Soul', is not merely a prayer or meditation-
state, but simply arises from an attitude to *all* the circumstances of life, even the most trivial and ordinary – an attitude
of relaxed openness, detachment and receptivity. We shall go

into this question more deeply later on, when we come to discuss the question of day-to-day spiritual life and how it is to be lived. For the moment we should note simply that 'seeing the world from within God' is not such a freakish and extraordinary affair as we might be tempted to think at first. In fact, it may be that some of us, who have acquired some degree of detachment and awareness of God, already do it at times, though perhaps rather imperfectly and for rather short periods – and above all, without realizing consciously what it is that we are doing.

To bring this chapter to its close, we can now ask the question: how does the world look to God? And how will it look to us, once we start to see it through God's eyes?

We have already described the universe as an *echo* of God's voice. That is not a bad image in many ways, since it shows that the universe *depends* totally upon God. Unless the voice speaks, there is no echo; once the voice stops, the echo, too, dies away. Another favourite image for Eckhart is that of an *image* in a mirror. If I stand over a bowl of clear, still water, I shall see my face reflected in it. But if I move away, then the reflection vanishes; it depends for its existence on my remaining there. The universe, too, is a kind of reflection; it reflects God, and can only do so as long as God remains present. If he should move away even for an instant, the universe would immediately cease to exist. It exists only as a reflection. A reflection of what? Of God. But more importantly: a reflection *in* what? What is it in the universe which reflects God back? The answer is: nothing.

To return to our earlier simile: that of the echo-chamber. Why is it that a chamber is able to echo the sound made within it? Because of its *hollowness* and *emptiness*. To return to our second simile: why is it that a mirror is able to reflect a face looking into it? Again, because of its emptiness. If a picture, or a colour, or a design were painted on the surface of the mirror, it would reflect nothing. If our mirror is a bowl of water, then it is also important that the water should be quite still. If there are ripples on the surface, the reflection will be hindered from forming. Ripples give the surface of the water a character and shape of their own; therefore the water can no longer reflect a shape or character from outside. To be able to reflect means to be empty and without inherent character. That is what the universe is like. It is able to become an echo-chamber for the Word, a mirror for the face of God the Son, because it is itself inherently *characterless* and *empty*.

The Church teaches us that God created the world out of *nothing*. It is the nothingness in it which is the source of its many imperfections. All the sorrow, frustrations, suffering and destruction in the world come from this nothingness. The reason I quarrel with another person is because I am *not* him, and my interests are *not* his. It is the *not* which creates the quarrel. The reason fire burns my hand if I put my hand into it is because the fire is *not* my hand. If I *were* the other person, I would have no quarrel with him; if my hand *were* the fire, it would not be burned by it. All imperfections in the world spring from this element of nothingness in things; therefore Eckhart says: if you want to be free of suffering, get rid of *not*. Later on, I shall discuss how this is done. But for the moment we should simply notice this nothingness which is at the heart of the universe: this is what makes it changeable and perishable, full of instability, imperfection and suffering. Ultimately the reason why the universe is imperfect is because it is *not God*.

That is something we tend to forget when we ask the question: how could a good and wise God create an imperfect universe? We overlook the fact that if the universe were perfect, it would not be a universe at all – it would be God. We should try, then, not to be saddened too much by the imperfections of the world, which make its joys and beauties so fleeting, transient and insecure. Rather, we should try to accept these imperfections as springing from its nothingness, the emptiness, which lies at the heart of things. This is not easy to do, for the things of this world make such a powerful impression on us that they seem to be solid, enduring and permanent. They are not. They exist only in a fleeting, transitory way, depending upon the continued presence of God; in themselves they are absolutely nothing. 'All creatures are pure nothing. I do not say they are a trifle or they are anything: they are pure nothing. All creatures have no being, for their being consists in the presence of God . . . '[4]

4. Walshe, vol. 1, p. 284.

Yet the paradox is that this very nothingness and emptiness has also a positive value, because it makes it possible for the universe to reflect God and thus have a share, however fleeting and provisional, in his existence and goodness. It is the fundamental emptiness in things which makes them a mirror for God's face, an echo-chamber for his Word.

Thus, seen from the standpoint of God himself, the created universe has a dual and paradoxical character. It both is and is not. In itself it is emptiness and nothingness, but in God it has being and perfection. The wisdom-eye of God perceives these two aspects simultaneously. In contemplating the universe, God sees only what there is of himself in it – for, indeed, there is nothing else in it to see! He sees only his own reflection, and hears only his own Word. At the same time he knows that what is reflecting him is pure nothingness, what is echoing him is pure emptiness. The world exists, but not absolutely; it is good, but only relatively. And that is how the world will appear to us, too, once our wisdom-eye is open and we see the world as God sees it. We shall be moved by its beauty and splendour, but at the same time we shall see the emptiness and nothingness on which it is based, and we know that in the end only God is fully true and good, without any admixture of *nothing*. This vision of things creates the attitude of detachment – in Eckhart's German, *abgeschie-denheit* – which is not a state of cold aloofness or scorn, but simply of lucid and compassionate awareness, taking things at their true value, a value which is real, but not absolute.

Thus, standing within the Word, we come to understand and love properly the world which is the Word's echo. This is essentially a *joyous* understanding, because it gives us a sense of the *rhythm* inherent in things: birth and death, light and dark, growth and decline, gain and loss, breathing in and breathing out. Within God these two movements are simultaneous: the Son comes forth from the Father yet simul-taneously returns to him through the Holy Spirit. God goes out from himself yet remains always within. In the created universe it is different; going out and returning are not simul-taneous, but successive. In us this gives rise to a feeling of disillusionment and sorrow, so long as we remain spiritually asleep, tied to the temporal world in which nothing is perma-nent. But if we detach ourselves from the temporal world and

take up our stand within the Word, then the apparently
meaningless flux immediately comes together and makes
sense. The wearisome alternation of life and death, death and
rebirth, no longer oppresses us once we are freed from it, and
dwell in the Word for whom going out and coming in are one
everlasting reality. The underlying harmony of the universe
is audible to us now that we can hear the keynote on which
it is all based. As a modern poet has put it:

On whom Thy Name has set its seal,
From him all movement is unfurled:
He is the centre of the wheel,
He is the axis of the world.

Its beauty sways him yet cannot win him.
Transparent motion and poise and glance
Reveal the sanctuary within him
Through patterned trellises of dance.[5]

The created universe is governed by the law of rhythm, the
Law of the Dance, springing ultimately from the Creative
Word, who, through His eternal going out and returning, is
the Archetype of all rhythm. Once we are aware of that Word
within ourselves, once we tune into it, live within it, and act
from within it, then we can make sense of all the knowledge
and experience that life in the world brings us, for we have
the *key* to it all.

This shows us what is the matter with our modern philosophy, science, technology, art, and even (sometimes!)
theology. We try to understand the world – and even what
there is of God revealed in it – too much from the *outside*,
instead of from *within*. Observation, analysis, experiment,
description – collating facts and data, manipulating and
exploiting people and things – these operations are not necessarily wrong, and they do lead to a kind of knowledge, but
not the truest and deepest knowledge, because they miss the
foundation on which the whole edifice is based. That foundation
cannot be found by looking outside ourselves; it can only be
found by looking within. Once we have found the Word
within and sensed its rhythm there, then we can look out at
the world and sense it there too. The stone which our modern
builders reject is, in fact, the cornerstone of the arch.

5. Martin Lings, *The Heralds*, p. 13.

What would a science, a philosophy, a technology be like, which, while not abandoning the outward operations of observation, experiment and analysis, nevertheless remained firmly grounded upon awareness of the Word within, the source and meaning of all? At present that is a possibility which we are hardly able even to conceive. Yet it is surely a real possibility – if knowledge through the Word and in the Word, as Eckhart expounds it, is also possible.

In a later chapter I shall go more deeply into the question of how we can reach this state in which the Word is spoken in the Ground of the Soul, and what living and acting in the world is like for one in whom this has happened. But we cannot watch the enactment of this drama yet, for there is still an important character missing. This is the Incarnate Word, Christ the Redeemer. The Divine Word is not only spoken inwardly, in the silence of the Trinity, and outwardly, in the created universe; it is also spoken historically, in the person of Jesus, the carpenter of Nazareth. This has profound implications for our own spiritual life, so we must look into these in the chapter which follows.

6 *The Incarnate Word*

The Christian religion is a religion of the flesh. The human body is not merely a tiresome burden which we have to carry, a dark, heavy prison in which a radiant spiritual soul is locked up as a punishment until it gains release in death. It has a central part to play in our journey to God. Until we have experienced its tug, its weight and resistance, there is no spiritual life possible for us. There are lessons for us to learn, experiences for us to undergo, which can come to us only through the body.

How can we find God through and in the flesh? We cannot, unless God comes into the flesh to meet us. So far on our spiritual journey, under Eckhart's guidance, we have not sought God in this realm, but in other, apparently more sublime realms where we might more readily expect to find him. In the Ground of the Soul – yes, we might expect to meet him there, because it resembles his own Abyss of Godhead, the Silent Desert. In the outflowing of personal relations and creative activity in the world – yes, we might expect to meet him there, too, for it mirrors the mystery of his own personhood, the eternal communion and union of Father, Son and Spirit within the Trinity, flowing out into the creation of the universe which reflects his glory and echoes to his Word. But in the human body, with its endemic weakness and its proneness to suffering, needing to be continually fed, kept warm, shielded from hurt, cured from illness – are we going to expect God to come here to meet us and draw us to himself?

Fortunately he has done so already, in the Person of Jesus of Nazareth, called by his followers 'the Christ'. A spiritual path which ignored this fact, or failed to take it into account, would not be worth very much. However, this is not a criticism which could be fairly levelled at the path of Eckhart. This is not to say that such criticism has never been made; it has, but on the basis of insufficient familiarity with his writings and a too one-sided understanding of his teaching. Christ is certainly not an irrelevant, nor even a secondary figure in Eckhart's spiritual way; he stands right at the centre of it, and it makes very little sense without him. In him the element of *paradox*, which is intrinsic to this path, reaches its maximum concentration and tension.

We have seen plenty of this paradox already, while looking at the Christian Revelation through Eckhart's eyes. It has been encountering us at every turn. God goes out, yet remains within; is one, yet three; is present within the universe yet distinct from it. The universe we live in is everything, yet nothing; it reveals God, yet at the same time veils him; it is, yet at the same time is not. But it is in the *human* condition that the paradox becomes most acute. We are animals, begotten in a bed, and subject to all sorts of primitive and atavistic instincts, yet we have within us a spark of heavenly nature, and we are destined for union with God, the Ultimate Absolute. As the Psalmist says, we are gods yet we shall die like men (Ps 82:6). This is our own, personal paradox. That means that it is here, above all, that we must look to find God.

So it is here that God himself comes to meet us, as Jesus who is both man and God. In the Christ, God comes into our human world and makes his home there, right at the heart of the paradox. When we read today about the early heresies in the Church about who and what Jesus was, the endless and acrimonious disputes about whether he was God or man, born naturally or supernaturally, was two Persons or one, had one nature or two – it can all sound very silly and irrelevant, a mere dispute about words or names. To a large extent it *is* silly and irrelevant – unless we wake up to the fact that in arguing about Jesus we are really arguing about ourselves. The paradox of Jesus is our own paradox. Like the Jews of Jesus' own day, we find it 'mind-blowing' to be faced with someone who is both God and man. Yet is that so very remote from our own condition, that of 'gods who will die like men'? It is no accident that Jesus, when attacked by the Pharisees for calling himself the Son of God, quoted this very Psalm-text in his defence.[1] He was saying, in effect: if you find *me* impossible and incomprehensible, what are you going to think about yourselves?

Questions about Jesus are always, at the same time, questions about ourselves, because he is the *archetypal* human being, the basic human pattern which we are all more or less faithful copies of. If we want to know what it truly means to be human, Jesus is the supreme example and demonstration. That is why the pictures and concepts we have of him change down the centuries; the changes reflect our concepts about ourselves, which are also continually changing and being revised. An age which stresses the divinity of Jesus at the expense of his humanity – finding it hard to believe that he ate, drank, or suffered pain – is an age which has a faulty concept of what human beings are, and is unable to come to terms with the animal and physical elements in our make-up. An age which stresses the humanity of Jesus at the expense of his divinity – not an uncommon phenomenon in the twentieth century – is one which has lost sight of the transcendent, spiritual element in our human nature, which can find ultimate fulfilment only in God, freed from the limitations of space and time. A faulty or one-sided picture of Jesus is always, by implication, a faulty or one-sided picture of ourselves.

Jesus is supremely mysterious; but then, so are we. It may be, therefore, that the perfect christological dogma, the final definitive statement about who and what Jesus is, can never be achieved, any more than there can be a final and definitive statement about who and what human beings are. Some statements are better and more complete than others, but none can be perfect in the sense of giving full and exhaustive expression to the reality, because the reality ultimately transcends verbal expression. Once we stop seeing Jesus as a mystery, we also stop seeing ourselves as a mystery; and that means we have lost hold of the truth. In fact, this is not a bad test of how deep our understanding is of another person (a lover, parent, or friend, for example). We have only to ask: is this person still a mystery to me? Do I find, the more I get to know him, the more mysterious he becomes? If this is so, then the

1. John 10:34.

relationship is deep and truthful, founded on real love and understanding. We can apply the same test to ourselves, and to our understanding of ourselves. Do I think I now know myself fully, so that I can predict exactly how I will react in a given situation? Do I have complete and detailed knowledge of all my hidden desires, hopes, fears and potentialities? If I think that, then I can be sure my self-knowledge is, in fact, far from complete. It has hardly even started. Once I stop thinking that I *know* myself and others, then there is a chance that some real knowledge might start to grow.

'If you were blind,' said Jesus to the Pharisees, 'you would have no guilt. But now that you say: "we see", your guilt remains.'[2]

When we form a faulty concept of Jesus, and therefore, of ourselves, we shall always find, if we look into the matter closely, that the fault lies in our failure to come to terms with the essentially *paradoxical* nature of the truth. It is very hard to face the fact of a being who is both divine and human, spiritual and material, mortal and immortal. The temptation is always to simplify the picture, to get rid of the painful paradox by suppressing one of its components. A being who is wholly spiritual and divine will not be troubled by the humiliating worldly facts of suffering, weakness and death. A being who belongs entirely in this world can cheerfully get on with the task of improving his material environment without being distracted by irrelevant and disquieting thoughts about the 'beyond'. To accept *both* elements of the paradox, to recognize their truth, and to attempt to live them, is difficult and uncomfortable. It is not a task for the lazy, the complacent, the fanatical or the opinionated. It is, however, the only way to truth and life.

No one had a clearer awareness of the paradoxical nature of spiritual life than Eckhart; so it would have been very odd if he had taken no interest in the figure of Christ, who is, we might almost say, Archetypal Paradox. However, that interest is certainly there. The question is: how does Eckhart see the paradox of Christ, and what does that tell us about the paradox which is ours?

For Eckhart, the truth about Christ is centred first and

2. John 9:41.

foremost on the mystery of the *Incarnation*, the birth of God
as Man. He is well aware that the story does not stop there:
the child born in Bethlehem grew up to be a man who under-
went a baptism and empowering by the Spirit, who for a
number of years carried out a teaching and healing ministry,
and who was finally put to death by crucifixion and rose
again miraculously afterwards. References to all these events
are to be found in Eckhart's writings, especially the Latin
ones; but it is the Incarnation that seems to preoccupy him
most, for he homes in on it time and time again. It is the
birth of Christ, rather than the Crucifixion or the Resurrection, which seems to him to have primary importance, and it
is this which he refers to most frequently. He does not explain
the reasons for this preference; but they are not far to seek.
First of all, the Incarnation is, so to speak, the 'root' mystery,
the mystery of God coming into the world. Once this stunning
event has happened, the rest unfolds with a certain inevitability: the Light shining in the darkness causes the darkness
to resist and try to overcome it; but the ultimate outcome of
the struggle has to be the triumph of the Light. As the Fourth
Gospel says: 'The light shines in the darkness, and the darkness has not overcome it.' The second reason for Eckhart's
concentration on the Incarnation is more subtle, and is bound
up with his particular way of viewing the truths of Christian
revelation. His aim is above all *mystical*. This does not mean
that he is interested in trances, visions, ecstasies, weird
psychic events, or abnormal states of consciousness – he is
not. It means that he is concerned above all with *union*, how
God and Man can come together and become *one*. Now this
happens in two ways. First, God and Man are united in the
historical event which took place in Bethlehem 2000 years
ago. Secondly, they are united here and now in the mysterious
event which Eckhart calls the Birth of God in the Soul, or
the Speaking of the Word in the Ground of the Soul. The
historical Incarnation in the past, and the 'mystical' Incarnation in us, here and now, are two aspects, distinct but
inseparable, of one single mystery – the mystery of the union
or marriage between God and Man.

If God had not been born historically, in Bethlehem, as
Jesus Bar Joseph, he could not be born mystically, here and
now, in us. It is probably not even sufficient to say that the

historical event is the *cause* of the mystical one. They are really only distinct components of a single mystery which transcends space and time. Eckhart openly and persistently refuses to view the birth of Jesus from an exclusively 'historical' point of view. The meaning and importance of the Incarnation lies in the fact that it is *not* simply an event which occurred 2000 years ago, but one which can be, and is, re-enacted here and now. If it could not be, we would have no very pressing reason for being interested in it. As Eckhart himself says, in a German sermon:

> Why did God become man? – I would answer, in order that God may be born in the soul, and the soul be born in God. For that reason all the Scriptures were written. God created the world and all angelic natures: so that God may be born in the soul and the soul be born in God.[3]

Now we are in a position to see what is Eckhart's peculiar view of Christ, of who and what he is. We have already seen that a concept of Christ is also, by implication, a concept of ourselves, of humanity. What is Eckhart's concept of Christ? It is of one in whom God and Man are made one. What is his concept of Man? It is of a being capable of becoming one with God. Eckhart is really only developing the ancient formula of Irenaeus and Athanasius: God became Man so that Man might become God. God became Man 2000 years ago in Palestine; but that was only so that he could become Man here and now, in you and me, and so that you and I, here and now, could become God. The mystery of God's Incarnation is also the mystery of our deification. The far-off event in Bethlehem is truly fulfilled and understood only when it becomes a *present* reality, enacted within ourselves, uniting us with God *now*.

This is Eckhart's answer to a problem which perplexes many of us today, namely: how to make Christ 'relevant' to modern people and to the modern world? As the Founder of our religion, invested with divine wisdom and power, he can appear very remote and distant from us, and thus cease to be an effective force or influence in our lives. A common modern solution to this problem is to concentrate on the Incarnation as an *historical* event, and to try to understand

3. Walshe, vol. 1, p. 215.

Jesus in terms of his historical context, by researching the cultural, political, social and religious conditions in which he lived and worked, and thereby trying to deduce how he would talk and act if he were born into our world today. It is not necessarily a mistake to approach Jesus from this point of view; it can, and does, yield some very positive results. For example, by showing how Jesus challenged the religious and social assumptions of his day, allying himself with the poor and rejected against the rich and well-established, we can be spurred on to help our own poor and underprivileged, and to question some of our own comfortable assumptions.

That this approach is yielding much fruit in many parts of the world today is surely beyond question. It is easy to see, also, and rather interesting, how this approach reflects our modern concept of ourselves. We are becoming more inter- ested in the historical Christ because we are coming to see ourselves, too, as essentially historical creatures. Man is an historical animal; therefore Jesus, the supreme Man, is also supremely historical. The influence of Marx has done a lot to shape our thinking on these matters, for he is perhaps the most powerful single factor in bringing about our modern concept of ourselves as engaged in history, moulded by history, making history. Yet, as we saw earlier, there is no final and definitive statement about Man, any more than there is one about Jesus. All statements, however truthful, are always imperfect and fall short of the total truth. The difficulties with the historical view are easy enough to see if we stand back and look at it in perspective – not an easy thing to do, nor even right, perhaps, for dedicated priests working hard in the slums of South America. The difficulty is that no two periods of history are really alike: the Palestine of Jesus' day, under the Roman rule, presented a combination of political, social and cultural conditions which have no exact parallel at the present time. So if we really find the 'historical' Jesus we are looking for, he might turn out to be rather remote and alien in many ways. He wore strange clothes, spoke an extinct language, thought and felt in terms very different from ours. He championed the poor, certainly, but were the 'poor' the same as our poor? Were they what we today would call the 'proletariat'? Was Jesus really a 'revol- utionary', as we today would understand that term?

None of this is meant to be an attack upon or criticism of the historical view of Jesus, or of the historical view of Man, which is a feature of our own time and has its important part to play in our own history. But it is important to remember that *all* views of Jesus and of ourselves are relative and partial, because if we do, that will help us to remain open to other, rather different views, which may also have their own value – even for our own time.

Eckhart's answer to the question of Jesus' 'relevance' is the exact opposite of ours. Instead of stressing the historical element, he deliberately underplays it. This has brought him some rather sharp criticism from certain modern thinkers who champion the historical view and find it hard to see the value of any other. But before we dismiss Eckhart's view as irrelevant, we ought to pause and bear a couple of things in mind. First, Eckhart is not *denying* that Jesus is an historical figure; he knows he is, and says so in a number of places. Second, if he does not see Jesus as being *primarily* and *essentially* historical, that is because he does not see Man as primarily historical either. We live in history, as Jesus did, but our ultimate fulfilment and meaning are not to be found there, but in God, who is not 'historical'. God may be Lord of History, but he is not contained in history, still less identified with it. It is space and time which make history, and God transcends space and time. So, indeed, do we, when we are true to ourselves.

It is perhaps worth expanding these two points a little, because they have some important implications for our own spiritual situation today. Eckhart is often described, rightly or wrongly, as a 'mystic', and a 'Neoplatonist'. There is an element of truth in these labels, but we must not take them as implying that Eckhart disbelieves in the historical Incarnation of Christ, or thinks it unimportant. He knows perfectly well that Jesus was born at a definite time in human history, in a context of Jewish religion, race and culture, which had been specially prepared for his coming. Eckhart explains this in his great Latin commentary on the Gospel of St John, where, expounding the text 'He came unto his own, and his own received him not', he remarks:

In the literal sense he [St John] means to say . . . that the Word

took flesh specifically among the race of Judah whose inheritance
was the Divine sayings and to whom had been given the Law
wherein Christ and His Incarnation and similar things were
prefigured. The people of that same God, the sheep of his pasture,
him they refused to accept in faith.[4]

It is true that Eckhart is here expounding only the 'literal'
sense of the text, implying that there are other, deeper meanings which he will examine in a moment – meanings which
are, of course, 'mystical', concerned with the birth of God
now, in you and me. But a literal sense is nevertheless a
true sense; it is not one which can be denied or waived as
unimportant. Eckhart does not intend to deny it or waive it.
Some people today, particularly of a 'mystical' or 'transcendental' bent, take the view that it does not matter very much
whether Jesus really existed or not, historically. It is sufficient
that he should have a merely mythological existence, as an
example and a spur to human aspirations. This is not
Eckhart's view at all. For him it is important that God, in
Jesus, actually entered human history, because that enables
him to lead us out of it! If God had not entered our world of
time and space, there would be no possibility of our transcending time and space. Until Jesus came, the historical
world was a prison; now it is the antechamber of heaven. But
this would not be so unless he had actually come.

So now we find ourselves faced with a very teasing and
typically Eckhartian paradox: yes, it is important that Jesus
existed historically, because it stops us from taking history
too seriously, and from thinking of ourselves as *essentially*
historical beings. Jesus enters history so as to free us from
history. History was one of the things Jesus died to on the
cross, and transcended at the resurrection. That means that
we should die to it and transcend it as well. We shall need
to look into this matter more closely in a later chapter, when
we come to deal with the question of our daily life in the
world and how to live it. But for the moment we need to
try to understand more clearly the curious paradox whereby
Eckhart, precisely by *not* stressing the 'historical' figure of
Jesus, actually makes him more 'relevant' to our own time –
and, indeed, to all times.

4. *Latin Works*, vol. 3, 5.89, 104, 12–16 (author's translation).

Why is it that there is a constant danger of Christ becoming a remote and intangible figure, unconnected with our daily life and concerns? Because we tend to see him exclusively as an *external* figure, outside ourselves; and anything which is external to us is perishable, changeable, and almost certain to be lost by us eventually. The only things which are truly relevant to us, which touch our lives at the centre, are things which are *internal*, part of our very being, and are therefore always with us, incapable of being lost through any kind of external accident. Christ is, or should be, that which is most central and internal in us. He is first and foremost a real and powerful force and agent *within ourselves*, rather than something external to ourselves. Being internal, and continually active within us, his power to heal and transform is practically unlimited. Jung, we may remember from an earlier chapter, saw the importance of this very clearly. One of his most serious criticisms of modern Christianity is that it tends to externalize Christ too much, and a Christ who is outside us can never heal that which is inside us, that which is deep, internal and private. Jung saw Christ primarily as a force within the human mind, and therefore real, potent and entirely 'relevant'. Furthermore, since Christ is always present and active within the human mind or psyche, there is no danger of his becoming outmoded or remote. The inner world of the human heart is only to a certain extent modified and altered by historical change, the rise and fall of cultures and empires. In its deepest and most central realms, things change very little, if at all – the needs and aspirations of humankind at this level are always the same, and do not change fundamentally from one historical epoch to another. So if Jesus, the Christ, is to be 'relevant' to us in the truest and most permanent sense, it is in this deepest and most inward part of ourselves that we must try to find him, rather than in the Galilee of 2000 years ago. Galilee, under the Roman Empire, is now lost to us, and is only partly reconstructable through archaeology and documents; but the inner core of ourselves remains present, so long as we have life and consciousness, and can never be lost. A Christ who dwells here really is a treasure which no thief can steal, an unshakable rock on which to build our lives.

But when God became Man in Bethlehem, 2000 years ago,

did he really enter this inner realm of the human heart? We know that he took on human flesh, but did he also take on this most secret and inward part of ourselves, which Eckhart calls the Ground of the Soul, nameless and transcendent, above space, time and personality, reflecting the nameless, transcendent eternity of God himself? In Eckhart's view, this is precisely what Christ did do. This, in fact, was the real Incarnation, much more 'real', in the strictest sense, than the taking on of flesh and blood, and of a particular cultural and historical situation. In the Person of God the Son, as Jesus, the carpenter of Nazareth, God entered the Ground of the Soul – that inner sanctum common to all human beings in all periods of history – and has remained there ever since.

That Eckhart considers this descent of God into the Ground of the Soul as the real Incarnation, is beyond reasonable doubt. He states this clearly in a number of places. For example, in a German sermon, commenting on the text 'God . . . sent His only begotten Son into the world' (1 Jn 4:9), he remarks of the word 'world': 'By this we must understand the great world into which the angels look.'[5]

An astonishing interpretation, very different from what we are used to! What does he mean by this 'great world into which the angels look'? He means the Ground of the Soul, which is nameless, transcendent, above space and time, which has kinship with God and in its deepest part is higher even than the angels. A further characteristic of this 'Ground' or 'great world' is that *it is the same in all of us*. This is something we need to ponder on a little more, in order to grasp more clearly what the Incarnation is about and how it affects us here and now.

The Ground of the Soul is, in one sense, that in us which is most intimate and private. I cannot communicate what is in mine to someone else, nor guess fully what is in his; even the sincerest 'words' do not express the whole reality. Yet in another sense the ground is not private at all; it is what we all have in common! Another teasing paradox. What must I do to get into my own Ground? I have to strip away the 'images'. I have to let go of all that I normally consider as 'myself', all the external part of my nature which is

5. Walshe, vol. 1, p. 110.

conditioned by outward circumstances, all my individual habits of mind, patterns of behaviour, assumptions and expectations. But if I do that, I shall have let go of all that is *distinctively* me, all that separates and distinguishes me from other people. In the Ground of the Soul there is indeed no male or female, Jew or Greek, no Tom, Dick or Harry: there is only a serene, naked openness and receptivity to God, and that is no different in me from what it is in someone else. At this level all distinctions between human beings fade away; at this level they are all one.

When Eckhart is considering the Ground of the Soul as that which unites us, when we are at our highest level, as that which we all have in common, when we are at our loftiest and truest, he has another term for it: he calls it 'universal human nature'. Again, an astonishing and unexpected use of words! When we talk about 'human nature' we usually mean our weakness, frailties and inconsistencies. 'It's only human nature', we say, if someone gives in to a particularly juicy temptation, or falls under a particularly heavy burden. Sometimes we use it in a slightly higher sense, talking, for example, of 'the essential goodness of human nature'. Yet Eckhart's use of the term, though startling, has a lot to be said for it. 'Human nature' is, for him, that which we are when we are at our best and truest. And when are we at our best and truest? When we are detached from self and creatures, when we are totally humble, receptive, and open to God. We are, essentially, creatures capable of union with God; this is the deepest truth that can be said about us. Therefore we are most ourselves, most human, when we are in this state, in the Soul's Ground. We are also most human then in the sense that we are most one with each other; there is no more Tom, Dick or Harry, names which create division and differences of interest; there is only a nameless, formless state of being which is the same in us all. We are no longer individual human beings; we are simply *human*.

Many people reading this book may protest at this point: 'But this entry into the Ground of the Soul is very difficult, and even impossible, for most people most of the time! So how can we say that it is being truly human, that it is true human nature? From our point of view it is not human; it is inhuman . . .' The answer is that it is only because we have become used to living a falsehood that we can no longer recognize the truth about ourselves, even when it stares us in the face. Receptivity and openness to God in the Soul's Ground are, in fact, what we were created for; to be like this is to be human in the truest sense; and if we cannot see it so, that is because our normal, everyday lives are lived mainly on a *subhuman* level. What we call 'normality' is in fact abnormality and sickness. It is a diseased state, which prevents us from being our true selves.

It is precisely this disease that Christ cures through his Incarnation. In becoming Man, he becomes *true* Man, one in whom the potentialities of the human state are actually realized. Jesus is a creature of flesh and blood like us; he has a human body, heart and emotions, and is therefore subject to all the temptations and weakness which that implies. But, being the supremely normal Man, rather than an abnormal one, these fleshly frailties do not prevent Him from being able to do what human beings are supposed to do – to cast aside these creaturely limitations and plunge into the mystery of God in the Soul's Ground. In his treatise on Detachment, Eckhart tells us that Christ, in the garden of Gethsemane and on the cross, suffered very intensely in his 'outer man' – that is, as a concrete, fleshly human individual – but remained totally detached and united with God in his 'inner man' which is the Soul's Ground. Since he has done this, it is now possible for us to do it too. In the Incarnation of Christ, God took on 'human nature', entering the Ground of the Man, Jesus. That Ground is common to us all, and Christ is still present within it. If we enter the Ground of the Soul, we shall encounter Christ, God the Son.

Not only shall we encounter the Son; we shall also *become* the Son ourselves; we shall share in the union which the Son has with the Father, the Spirit and the Divine Ground, the Abyss, the Silent Desert. If we strip away from ourselves all that is accidental, relative and individual in ourselves, we shall attain that 'universal human nature' which has been united to Christ, and the Incarnation will thus become a present reality for us, here and now, in our lives.[6]

I say that human nature and man are different. Humanity in

6. Clark and Skinner, p. 167.

itself (i.e. at its deepest and truest, when it is most genuinely itself) is a noble thing; that which is highest in human nature has likeness to the angels and kinship with the Godhead. It is possible for me to obtain the greatest union which Christ had with the Father, provided that I am able to lay aside everything 'which is of this and that' and provided that I can take to myself universal human nature. Therefore all that God ever gave to his only begotten Son he has also given to me as perfectly as to him and not less . . . [7]

Now we can see what kind of importance Eckhart thinks Christ had for us. Christ is of central importance because in him is enacted the central mystery of the union between God and Man. This happens through the Incarnation, which has a double aspect. On the one hand, God incarnates in the flesh, as Jesus of Nazareth, born into a particular historical situation. This is what we might call the 'outward' aspect of the Incarnation. Far more important, however, in Eckhart's view, is the 'inward' aspect, whereby God enters universal human nature, the transcendent Ground which is common to all human beings wherever they are in space or time. This aspect is more important because it touches us here and now in the deepest core of ourselves, and transforms our lives.

Concepts of Jesus are also concepts of ourselves. If in Jesus there was an 'inner' and an 'outer' man, so there must be in us. Redemption, salvation, must take both aspects into account, and we, today, in our own spiritual lives, must take them into account. We experience the 'outward' Incarnation by recalling it, through the Church, the sacraments, the Scriptures, the endeavour to live a virtuous life. By these means the outer man is purified, and is freed from his dependence on external stimuli and conditioning. But there has also to be an encounter with the 'inner' Incarnation, by detachment from the external world and by entry into the Ground of the Soul. This is by far the most important aspect, because it is through this alone that real change, transformation and union with God are achieved. The Incarnation then ceases to be merely a historical event in the past which is 'recalled' and applied to our outer lives; it becomes a present event, here

7. *German Works*, vol. 2,5.15,14. (Author's translation; cf. Walshe, vol. 1, p. 94).

and now, which transforms our inner lives. Christ is an irre-
sistible force within us, uniting us with God at this very
moment.

It is often asked today whether our spiritual life should be
'God-centred' or 'Christ-centred'. Eckhart would answer: it
should be centred *on* God, *in* Christ. We should not see Christ
so much as an external figure of worship and devotion, but
as one with whom we are *already* united, the moment we enter
the Ground of the Soul. We then share in his relationship
with the Father; we are sons in the Son. And this, after all,
is in total harmony with the mind of the Church, whose
normal prayer is addressed *to* the Father, *through* the Son.
Jesus himself, too, during his earthly life, does not seem to
have encouraged his followers to pray to him, but to his
Father, who was now their Father too. Throughout the New
Testament prayer seems to be addressed primarily to the
Father, in the name of Jesus, or in Jesus. In this way we are
caught up into the inner life of the Trinity and become part
of it.

Therefore Eckhart does not encourage us to become
'Christ-centred' in the sense of being exclusively preoccupied
with the historical figure, the Aramaic-speaking Galilean
rabbi who wandered about ancient Palestine in a white robe.
He wants us rather to encounter Christ as a living, active
force within ourselves, in the present moment. The Church,
with her Scriptures and sacraments, will prepare us for this;
but even within the Church it is still possible, if we are not
careful, to remain stuck in a relatively external and superficial
encounter with Christ. We need to go further, and discover
the *inner* Christ. Rather than merely 'follow' Christ, or
'believe' in Christ, we *become* Christ. In becoming Christ, we
discover the essential paradox of his nature and ours: that we
are creatures of mortal flesh, yet destined for the immortal
life of spirit; that we are historical, born into space and time,
yet destined to transcend history, space and time. We see
that the paradox of Christ, the God-Man, is also our own
paradox, once we become one with him in the Soul's Ground.

But all this is still too theoretical. We still have not faced
the question: how, exactly, are we to go about 'entering the
Ground' and experiencing the Incarnation here and now?
This is the subject of the next chapter.

7   The Way and the Goal

As our involvement with Eckhart increases, and as we penetrate more deeply into his thought, we shall find two questions pressing in on us with increasing urgency. First: what exactly is the *goal* which he is leading us to? And second: what is the *way* which he wants us to tread in order to get there? It is high time now for us to bring these two questions into focus, and to attempt some sort of clear answer to them.

Concerning the first, the question of the goal, there are certain misunderstandings which tend to fog the issue, and they must be cleared away at once. The biggest misunderstanding springs from words such as 'mystic' and 'mystical'. For us today these words conjure up a number of meanings and associations, most of which have nothing to do with what Eckhart is teaching us, and which are liable to lead us astray if we trust in them. Once we are told that Eckhart is a 'mystic' and that his teaching is 'mystical', our immediate reaction is likely to be: 'Oh, but I'm not a mystic.' Having decided, perhaps rightly, that we are not mystics, we then go on to decide, tragically, that Eckhart's way is not for us. This is a bad mistake, and we must be careful not to make it. The mistake springs from the interpretations and meanings which we read into words. As a matter of fact, it is rather a debatable question whether Eckhart's teaching is 'mystical'. If we decide to call it that, we shall need to be very clear about what we understand that term to mean.

One current meaning of the word 'mystic', for example, is hopelessly wide of the mark when applied to Eckhart. This is the use of the word to describe events or powers of a magical or psychic kind. Eckhart is emphatically not teaching us to 'develop our psychic powers', such as telepathy, clairvoyance, divination, levitation or even 'psychic healing'. He knows that such powers exist, and occasionally he refers to them; it would have been surprising if he did not, for such things were common in medieval Europe, and Eckhart likes to use images drawn from the life he knows. But this is precisely the point: these are *images* and *illustrations;* they are not the teaching itself, not what the teaching is all about. He talks, for example, about the 'magical' power inherent in certain plants and precious stones – thought in the Middle Ages to be due to the influence of the planets. But this is just an image for the way in which the human soul is 'empowered' when it is united with God. He also talks about the secret science of alchemy, which seeks to effect the mysterious transformation of the elements. But this, too, is only an image for the way in which the soul is transformed and ennobled through its union with God. He makes a brief reference to experiences of precognition or foreknowledge, even admitting to having had some such experiences himself from time to time; but here again he mentions this only in passing as an example of some of the 'side-effects' which can occur when the grace of God is at work in us. It is the grace of God, and how we are to open ourselves up to it, that concerns him; the 'supranormal' side-effects have no intrinsic interest or importance at all. So anyone embarking on Eckhart's 'mystical' path in the belief that he is going to learn some kind of wizardry, will be gravely disappointed. Eckhart has little in common with Aleister Crowley.

What distinguishes Eckhart's path most of all from that of the magician or occultist is that it is not aimed at the acquisition of *power*. Despite much talk in occultist circles about the quest for 'knowledge', it is hard to avoid the impression that what is in fact being searched for is not knowledge so much as power; knowledge is only useful for the power which it brings. Is Eckhart interested in acquiring power, in the sense of being able to *control* people or events? Not in the least. His path is the path of Christ; it aims at the *renunciation* of power. Christ was at his most 'kingly' when on the Cross; and Eckhart, too, knows that the way to gain the world is to renounce it. Whatever one may think of Aleister Crowley, not even his best friends could claim that his path was one of renunciation. He and Eckhart part company radically on this point.

All this discussion, however, springs from a rather crude and inexact use of the word 'mystical'. We need to look next at a more serious and profound meaning, which nevertheless should not be applied to Eckhart without certain grave reservations. This is the use of the word 'mysticism' to mean religious *experience*. A mystic, according to this view, is one who, instead of merely *believing* in God, actually *experiences* God. God is thus an almost tangible and palpable reality in the mystic's life; he is not merely a theological or philosophical theory.

Now we are getting closer to the truth of the matter, and so, inevitably, we find ourselves faced with a teasing paradox. This is only to be expected in the course of any serious spiritual way, and it is very much to be expected with Eckhart. In one sense it is quite right to say that he is leading us to an 'experience of God'. But that expression, too, is usually surrounded by a fog of misunderstanding which we shall have to dispel if the expression is to be really applicable to the case in hand. The situation is perhaps best summed up by saying: yes, Eckhart is leading us to an 'experience', but not, perhaps, to 'experience' as we would normally be inclined to understand that term.

What fogs the issue for us in the twentieth century is our proneness to what we might call the 'trip-mentality'. The haste, confusion, fragmentation, drabness and meaninglessness of modern life leads us to seek escapes in momentary experiences of bliss, brought about by the appropriate music, or films, drugs, sex, or even Eastern meditational techniques. What we are after, in other words, is a 'trip'. We want a thrilling experience of ecstasy which will relieve the drabness of our lives. This kind of desire is no doubt natural enough; but if we are not careful it will lead us to a seriously distorted notion of what 'spiritual life' is. We shall consider our spiritual life as healthy and genuine only to the extent that it provides us with these 'trips'. If these are not forthcoming, we shall be tempted to conclude that we have somehow gone wrong. In other words, we are putting our spirituality on the same level as pop music, marijuana, or even the latest brand of washing-powder; we expect *results* from it as soon as possible, preferably, and at the least personal cost and sacrifice to ourselves.

If we are going to talk about Eckhart's path as 'mystical', it is vital to realize that it is not concerned with 'trips', or with results of any tangible or obvious kind. Neither is it about what we call today the 'expansion of consciousness'. It is not concerned with trying to induce abnormal states, either blissful or otherwise; it is concerned with trying to develop within ourselves a certain *attitude* which is healthy, realistic and life-giving, and will remain constant within us during *all* states of consciousness, normal or abnormal, pleasant or unpleasant. This attitude is one of renunciation, of detached 'letting go', of open and relaxed receptivity to the present moment and whatever it contains. We are not being invited to cultivate certain experiences and to shun others, but to remain open to all of them, clinging to none, refusing none, but merely accepting them when they are there, and not pining after them when they are not there. Rather than talking about 'expansion' of consciousness, we should talk of 'breaking through' consciousness; that is, finding within ourselves some inner centre of stability and unity which remains intact throughout the manifold fluctuations of conscious states. 'Breaking through' – in German *durchbrechen* – is a genuine Eckhartian expression, occurring often in his writings; but the most zealous seeker would find it hard to discover in his works any word equivalent to our 'mind-expanding'. A person who is constantly hankering after unusual mental states has certainly wandered from the path of Eckhart; whereas one who can live serenely with normal mental states, however dull or unpleasant these may sometimes be, is more likely to be on the right track.

Yet, having said all this, we are not entirely wrong in saying that the path we are being taught is an *experience* of a certain kind, with quite tangible and perceptible effects. Certainly it affects our inner life, in the Soul's Ground, because it is here that the mysterious event occurs which is called 'the Birth of God in the Soul' or 'the Speaking of the Word in the Soul'. Eckhart tells us this on almost every page of his writings. But it also affects our outer life, even our physical life, which Eckhart calls the 'lower powers', meaning feeling, imagination, bodily senses, perhaps even bodily strength and vitality. Eckhart speaks of 'light', 'shooting down into the lower powers', when the Birth occurs. So it is clear that some sort of experience is envisaged. But what sort? That is the question.

Nearly everyone who writes or talks about Eckhart today seems to take it for granted that the great 'mystical' event, the Birth of God in the Soul, is a *prayer* or *meditation* experience. If this is so, then it obviously requires the appropriate external setting: solitude, silence, stillness of body and mind. But is this really what Eckhart is talking about? I, personally, do not think so. It may be a *part* of what he is talking about, but only a part, and not necessarily even the most important part. That is what makes it all the more interesting and valuable for us, for only a small minority of people today – as also, no doubt, in Eckhart's own day – are able to obtain regularly the external conditions of silence and solitude needed in order to reach the deeper meditational states taught by St John of the Cross, or Augustine Baker, or the great yogic teachers of Hinduism and Buddhism. So we need to ask ourselves now: when Eckhart speaks of the Birth of God in the Soul, what exactly is he talking about? If it is not a prayer or a meditation experience, what is it?

Much of what he says does lend itself, at first sight, to being interpreted as an introverted state, of the type gained in meditation or in certain forms of wordless, imageless prayer. His language is reminiscent of *The Cloud of Unknowing*, and other exponents of what is called the Negative Way. In *The Cloud* we are taught to be still and quiet, not to try to form words or pictures in the mind, but to plunge into a mental darkness in which no thoughts or images are formed, and in which nothing stirs save a naked, blind motion of the will, a fiery dart cleaving the darkness, reaching out to we know not what. Now there can be little doubt that Eckhart would have entirely approved of such an exercise, for those who are capable of it. It is highly likely that he practised it himself; it is certain that his disciple, Tauler, did; and it would also have been the regular practice of the enclosed Dominican nuns to whom Eckhart, as Provincial, had to minister and give spiritual direction. Persistence in this kind of practice, especially when accompanied by silence, solitude and various forms of self-denial, is quite likely to lead to momentary experiences of ecstasy or illumination, in which the heart is suddenly pierced by what the author of *The Cloud*

calls 'a beam of ghostly light'. Much of what Eckhart says
about the Birth of God in the Soul seems to describe this sort
of experience.

> . . . the very best and noblest attainment in this life is to be silent
> and let God work and speak within. When the powers (i.e. of
> thought, imagination and sensation) have been completely with-
> drawn from all their words and images, *then* the Word is spoken.
> Therefore He (God) said: 'In the midst of the silence the secret
> word was spoken into me.' And so, the more completely you are
> able to draw in your powers to a unity and forget all those things
> and their images which you have absorbed, and the further you
> can get from creatures and their images, the nearer you are to
> this and the readier to receive it.[1]

This sounds like a typical account of an imageless prayer or
meditation state as taught by exponents of the Negative Way.
But it is not. If we interpret it to mean this, we immediately
find ourselves stumbling over many passages in which
Eckhart seems to be saying the opposite; in which he speaks
rather ironically about people who get 'hooked' on solitary
meditation, who think they will never approach union with
God unless they withdraw from the world and plunge into
contemplation. An example of this 'anti-meditation' case is
his extraordinary sermon on the gospel story of Martha and
Mary,[2] in which he contradicts everything that is normally
said by preachers on this theme, and also seems to contradict
everything that he normally says himself about withdrawing
from creatures and their images, to let the Word be spoken
in the Ground of the Soul. It has been traditional, until fairly
recent times, to interpret this story as a parable about the
respective merits of Action and Contemplation. Martha, who
is busy about many things, and chides her sister for not
helping, represents Action; Mary, who sits quietly at Jesus'
feet and drinks in all his words, represents Contemplation.
Jesus gently reproves Martha for criticizing her sister, saying
that Mary, far from wasting her time, has 'chosen the better
part, which shall not be taken from her'. What could be
clearer? Obviously Jesus is maintaining the priority of
Contemplation over Action, saying that it is better to remain

1. Walshe, vol. 1, pp. 6–7.
2. See Walshe, vol. 1, p. 79.

in rapt meditation and union with God than to plunge into active works, however charitable. And from this we can deduce a whole theory of 'states of life', saying that it is better to be an enclosed monk or nun than a busy housewife or banker. But Eckhart, surprisingly though characteristically, turns this whole traditional interpretation on its head, maintaining that the true heroine of the story is not Mary but Martha. Mary, for him, is the prototype of the kind of person who has got 'hooked' on the 'meditation trip', who has become so absorbed in her private contemplative ecstasies that she refuses to emerge from them even when there is serious practical work to be done for which her help is needed. Martha, on the other hand, is represented as a much more mature person, and much further advanced in the spiritual life: she knows about contemplative rapture but does not cling to it; what matters to her is to serve God *in the way the present occasion demands*, and if the present demand is for action, rather than contemplation, that is all right by her. Eckhart's interpretation here may well seem to many people to be rather mischievous and perverse. Perhaps it is. But it is probably his clearest and fullest statement to the effect that union with God at the highest and deepest level is not something which happens necessarily in situations of withdrawal and 'inwardness'; on the contrary, it is perfectly compatible with extreme busyness. This argument, in the Martha and Mary sermon, does not by any means stand alone as an isolated case; anyone who reads Eckhart at all extensively will have no difficulty in finding many more examples, especially in the *Talks of Instruction*.

So now we really are on the perplexing knife-edge of a paradox; withdrawal from creatures while being busy over them, stillness of mind while full of distractions, freedom from images while having our head full of them! Who can make sense of this? And for good measure, let us add another paradox: we are being called to an experience which is not an experience, a union with God which is perceptible yet utterly ineffable, ecstatic yet not a 'trip', extraordinary yet totally normal. Furthermore, it is something which is both serious and funny. Serious the Birth of God in the Soul certainly is; it is what human life is all about, it is what we are created for. Yet Eckhart continually makes jokes about it; there are very few sermons in which he does not liven his discourse with touches of humour, or illustrate his point with extraordinary and even grotesque examples.

Obviously we must make some sort of attempt to sort out this incredible tangle – recognizing, of course, that in the last analysis it cannot be sorted out. It is intrinsically paradoxical and cannot be 'resolved' without falsifying it; yet we must try to find some way of getting into it rather than remain perpetually baffled and perplexed on the outside.

What we are being faced with here is the application to our own deepest and most personal spiritual life of the great formula we encountered earlier: going out, yet remaining within. God remains eternally transcendent and enclosed within the Divine Abyss, the Silent Desert; yet he simultaneously emerges from this to generate the Divine Persons of the Trinity and to create the world. The world, too, 'goes out yet remains within'. It is conceived, first and foremost, by the mind of God, in the Divine Word within the Trinity, and there it is not different from God himself, for what is *in* God *is* God. Yet it is also 'spoken forth' or made manifest as the created universe which we know, and perceive as something different from God, though we would be sorely taxed to explain how anything which is different from God can exist at all. Finally we encounter our own paradox: we have to 'go out', occupying ourselves with creatures, images and works, while remaining somehow 'within', free from images, creatures and works, in solitary union with the One in the Soul's Ground. How can we achieve this extraordinary feat? What do we have to *do* in order to live out this paradox, and experience the Birth of God in the Soul's Ground?

The answer is that the key to this mystery is not a *practice* but an *attitude*. It is not a matter of whether we pray or weed the garden, whether we retire to a hermitage or drop into the local pub for a glass of beer and a chat. It is a matter of *how* and *why* we do these things; it is a question of attitude. What is this attitude? It is that which is called by Eckhart by the German word *abgeschiedenheit*: normally translated as 'detachment'. This translation does not really do justice to the meaning, but we had better keep it since it would be hard to find a better one. What then, exactly, is this 'detachment'?

Since this is such a crucial question, we had better let Eckhart answer it himself in his own words:

> Now you might ask, what is detachment, since it is so noble in itself? Here you should know that true detachment is nothing other than this: the spirit stands as immovable in all the assaults of joy or sorrow, honour, disgrace or shame, as a mountain of lead stands immovable against a small wind. This immovable detachment brings about in man the greatest similarity with God. For if God is God, He has it from His immovable detachment, and from this detachment He has His purity, His simplicity and His immutability. And therefore, if man is to become like God, as far as a creature can possess similarity to God, it must be by means of detachment. It is this that leads man to purity and from purity to simplicity and from simplicity to immutability. And these things bring about a certain similarity between God and man. But this similarity must take place through grace, for grace draws man away from temporal things and purifies him from all transient things.[3]

This is an extremely important passage, containing the key to the Eckhartian way. Therefore it is important to look at it closely and make sure that we understand it properly.

First of all, is it true that the practice of this detachment is the way to get into the Soul's Ground and attain union with God? Yes, it is, for Eckhart has said: 'This immovable detachment brings about in man the greatest similarity with God', and 'as far as a creature can possess similarity to God, it must be by means of detachment'. To possess similarity to God is the same thing as to attain union with God, for the Way of Knowledge works through likeness, as we saw in Chapter 2 of the present book; we come to resemble that which we know, and the more we resemble it, the more we truly know it, and the more we truly know it, the more we are one with it. So if detachment makes us similar to God, then it is the road to our union with God. In this same extract there are many other statements which show that entry into the Soul's Ground is achieved by detachment. We saw earlier how the Ground of the Soul resembles God's transcendence, the Silent Desert of Godhead, by being likewise nameless, transcendent, raised above space and time, single, inviolate,

3. Clark and Skinner, pp. 163–4.

unified in itself. Now we hear Eckhart saying that detachment 'leads man to purity and from purity to simplicity and from simplicity to immutability'. All these are qualities ascribed to the Transcendent Godhead and its mirror-image, the Ground of the Soul. Through detachment, then, we enter the nameless depths of ourselves which call out to the nameless depths in God, as in the text of the Psalm: 'Deep calls unto deep'. Furthermore, to unite with God means stripping away the images, peeling away the projections which veil our true nature and God's. This is surely what is meant by the 'purity' mentioned in the passage quoted on page 95, the purity which is gained through detachment. Do we want to plumb our own depths, and the analogous depths of God? Then detachment is the way to do it.

Now, to revert to our earlier question: what, exactly, *is* detachment? This is very subtle, and easily misunderstood. It is true that Eckhart is giving us a definition here: ' . . . True detachment is nothing other than this: the spirit stands as immovable in all the assaults of joy or sorrow, honour, disgrace or shame, as a mountain of lead stands immovable against a small wind.' The trouble with this definition is that although it is very good up to a point, it does not cover the whole reality; it needs to be supplemented by other statements made by Eckhart elsewhere, otherwise we shall have a distorted and one-sided view of what it means. As it stands, it hardly makes detachment sound attractive. It may suggest rather an impressive quality which inspires respect, but hardly an attractive one which inspires love; it sounds somewhat cold, impersonal and aloof. It sounds Stoic rather than Christian; there is more of the 'stiff upper lip' about it than of the fiery, melting Way of Love taught by Jesus. But this is a false impression, which is immediately dispelled once we see this definition of detachment in the context of Eckhart's teaching as a whole. Detachment is not meant to be a cold and unfeeling thing. There is fire and passion behind it; the insatiable desire for God which reaches out to its goal and will not be fobbed off with anything less.

Why is it that detachment remains unaffected by 'the assaults of joy or sorrow, honour, disgrace or shame'? Because these are only fleeting, transient, temporal things; they are not God. It is the nature of the spiritual intellect to pierce through the veils to get at the Person behind them; to strip away the images to get at the reality; to rise above the creatures to find the Creator. It is only with regard to creatures that Eckhart wants us to practise detachment; there is no suggestion that we should be detached in our relations with God – on the contrary, where God is concerned we can be as fiery and passionate as we like, 'melting' and 'boiling' like the Persons within the Trinity.

Even so, some people may still find detachment a rather cold virtue, if it is a virtue at all. Granted that it allows us passion in our relations with God, it nevertheless implies great coldness and aloofness to the world surrounding us, that we fix our attention on our own private mystical quest and let the world go hang. Is this a truly Christian and compassionate attitude? What has it to do with the caring God of the Bible who *loved* the world, to the point of sending his Son to redeem it, the God who is passionately concerned with the fleeting, temporal world and its affairs? Surely the teaching of Julian of Norwich is better, who saw the world as a tiny nut in God's hand – an absurdly small and frail thing, yet none the less loved and cherished by God? Would it not be better for us to have a loving, outward-going attitude to the world, rather than shut ourselves up in the impregnable fortress of detachment?

The answer is that detachment does not require us to be shut off from the world in the sense of being indifferent to its sufferings or failing to recognize our responsibilities towards it. These sufferings are real, and our duty to relieve them as far as we can is also real. Therefore Eckhart says that if I am in a state of rapt, ecstatic meditation, and a poor man wants a bowl of soup from me, then the right thing is emphatically for me to leave my rapture and attend to my suffering fellow-man. What matters in my dealings with the world is that they should be entirely free from self-seeking. We have to be alert to the *demands* of the present moment, which may be very different from what we would like them to be. But the important thing is to be constantly seeking God in all that we do, trying to discern what he wants of us in a given situation, and doing it promptly, regardless of our personal likes or dislikes. It is this obedience to the Will of God, and indifference to our personal feelings, which constitutes true detachment. Once we have this, it makes no difference what we do: whether we pray or play football, retire to a hermitage or take up the running of a youth club. We can help the world by living an enclosed life of prayer and mortification, like Thérèse of Lisieux, or by living a life of active service to others, like Mother Teresa of Calcutta. What we do, and how we serve God, is not important; what matters is the surrender of selfish desire, and the ready, immediate response to God's demands as they present themselves to us here and now.

It is this realization that *it does not matter* what form our service to God takes, that constitutes the 'indifference' of detachment as defined by Eckhart in the passage quoted on page 95, its 'immovability' in all the 'assaults of joy or sorrow, honour, disgrace or shame'. We are not to be detached in the sense of being ungenerous and refusing to give ourselves; on the contrary, our self-giving has to be total. Detachment comes in only with regard to the *kind* of gift which may be required of us at any given time. Anyone who actually tries to practise this sort of detachment will soon find out how hard it is. To serve God in the way he actually wants us to serve him, rather than in the way we would like to serve him, is extremely difficult and mortifying. Often it is precisely when we feel the need for prayer and solitude that someone comes knocking on our door for help and guidance. Equally often it is precisely when we feel all aflame with apostolic zeal to transform the world and inaugurate the Kingdom by our strenuous activity, that we really need to withdraw and commune alone with God. Sometimes what we are called to do will be easy and pleasant; sometimes it will be difficult, painful, or even dangerous. That, too, should be a matter of indifference. From all this it is easy to see that detachment is a very strong, rather rugged virtue; yet no one could claim that it is cold or ungenerous. It requires, on the contrary, total, unconditional giving, limitless love. It requires that we have 'boiled' and 'melted' into the Will of God.

Right at the beginning of this book it was said that if we want to understand Eckhart's teaching fully, we must take it as a whole. We must be careful not to overstress any element to the point at which some other element, perhaps equally important, becomes obscured. This is particularly true in the matter of detachment. Detachment is not meant to stand on its own; at all times it should be accompanied by fiery striving. It was said earlier in this chapter that detachment is the proper attitude to creatures and means, and fiery striving is the proper attitude to God, the goal. This is what Eckhart seems to be saying. Yet there are some spiritual teachers who might want to take issue with him here and say that even with regard to God, the goal, our fiery striving needs to be tempered with detachment. Why? Because if we reach out to the goal too eagerly, we shall probably miss it. If we expect too much too quickly, we may end up with nothing at all. Also, our spiritual life is not simply a matter of our seeking God; it is also a matter of God seeking us. Sometimes the best policy is just to be still and wait. So in everything we do – our prayer, our work, our relations with others, and even our general spiritual quest – it is perhaps best always to balance striving with detachment, love with restraint.

There is quite a lot more to be said about the practice of detachment in our day-to-day life in the world. That can keep until the next chapter, which is concerned precisely with this. But for the moment we need to see how detachment, as we now understand it, affects the question of the Birth of God in the Soul, and whether this Birth is purely and simply a prayer-experience, or something wider.

Obviously it must be something wider. Union with God, detached from creatures and images, as Eckhart understands it, is not bound to any particular activity or state of consciousness. It is simply a matter of total renunciation, total surrender to the will of God. That surrender might, indeed, occur during prayer or meditation, but not necessarily so. It might occur when dealing with some importunate and apparently unreasonable demand put on us by someone else. But the more *free* we are from our personal moods, likes and dislikes, the more open and responsive we are to what is required of us at any given time, then the deeper we shall be settling into the Soul's Ground, and the closer we shall be coming to the Birth of God within ourselves, the awesome moment when self goes out and God comes in.

Whether the road to this leads through solitary meditation or through strenuous activity in the world will depend upon the person and the circumstances. It depends on what is blocking our union with God, what has to be surrendered for

the union to take place. If I have a compulsive urge to be
continually 'doing', manipulating other people and events,
'making my mark' in the world, then detachment may well
require me to drop all this, at least sometimes, and learn
simply to sit still and to *be* rather than to *do*. In our present
society and culture, which is rather feverish and over-active,
continually bombarding us with 'images', over-stimulating us
through the media, it is highly likely that we shall need to
practise some form of withdrawal and inner recollection, if
we are to develop any real spiritual life. But suppose the
opposite situation, in which I am 'hooked' on the 'meditation
trip', so overwhelmed by the blissful sensations I get from
prayer that I cannot bear to stop, that I find it impossible to
work up any interest in other people or their affairs? Then
detachment requires me to 'snap out of it' and do something
useful for someone else; because this is the only way I can
surrender the selfish clinging to inner pleasure which is
blocking my way to God.

Prayer and work, Action and Contemplation – these are,
when all is said and done, only creatures; they are not absol-
utes, they are not God. So to surrender to God, in detachment
from creatures and images, cannot be something which
happens only in prayer, and the Birth of God cannot be
simply a state of prayer. It must be a total inner turnover of
our attitude and awareness, which remains constant in *all*
that we do or leave undone.

We ought to end this chapter by asking the question: what
exactly is this Birth of God like, as an experience? Are there
any signs enabling us to know when it has occurred? Here it
is best to let Eckhart speak for himself:

I am often asked if a man can reach the point where he is no
longer hindered by time, multiplicity, or matter. Assuredly! Once
this birth has really occurred, no creatures can hinder you;
instead, they will all direct you to God and this birth. Take
lightning as an analogy. Whatever it strikes, whether tree, beast,
or man, it turns at once towards itself. A man with his back
towards it is instantly turned round to face it. If a tree had a
thousand leaves, they would all turn right side up towards the
stroke. So it is with all in whom this birth occurs, they are
promptly turned towards this birth with all they possess, be it
never so earthy. In fact, what used to be a hindrance now helps

you most. Your face is so fully turned towards this birth that, no matter what you see or hear, you can get nothing but this birth from all things. All things become simply God to you, for in all things you notice only God, just as a man who stares long at the sun sees the sun in whatever he afterwards looks at. If *this* is lacking, this looking for and seeking God in all and sundry, then you lack this birth.[4]

This passage is clear enough as it stands; but perhaps a few brief comments are in order.

There is a suggestion that the Birth is instantaneous and sudden, like a flash of lightning. Yet it is not transitory; it lasts, because it 'is no longer hindered by time, multiplicity or matter'. So if we are going to call it an experience of 'ecstasy' or 'rapture' it must be a kind of ecstasy very different from our ordinary worldly ecstasies, which do not last and which have the inevitable correlate – 'pain'. In our ordinary, unilluminated experience, joy and sorrow are complementary; they succeed each other; the existence of the one implies the existence of the other. But here we have something which is above the worldly alternation of opposites: a light which knows no darkness, a joy which no pain can extinguish.

Also, it is certainly an experience of the transcendent, of God, since Eckhart explicitly says so. Yet it is not world-denying. Our physical body, with all its passions and appetites, is no longer an obstacle but actually an aid; God now shines at us out of everything, however 'worldly' and 'earthy'. So it is a real Birth, a real Incarnation, in which God is encountered *in the flesh*. The great event of Bethlehem which we pondered over in the preceding chapter, has become a present and overwhelming reality; and the body is very much included in it.

Lastly, it is supremely paradoxical. It transcends time, yet it occurs in time; it transcends creatures, yet creatures help it and are a part of it; it is an experience of God, yet an experience of the world as well. Perhaps at this point it is best to say no more, but simply to ponder in silence and wait, in hope, for the time to come when the Birth occurs in us.

4. Walshe, vol. 1, p. 45.

8 The Glory of the Kingdom

Interpretations of Scripture are rarely based on purely external, objective criteria; they tend also to reflect the theological bias of their age. There is a gospel text which used to be translated 'the Kingdom of God is within you'.[1] That suggests some kind of inner, mystical event. Today translators prefer to render it as 'the Kingdom of God is among you', or 'in your midst'. That suggests a corporate event, one which does not merely occur privately in the individual soul but in the body of the believing community. There is no need for us to feel that we have to choose between these two renderings. Both express an important truth, for the Kingdom does have a double aspect; it is both inward and outward, individual and collective, private and shared. How we balance these two aspects in our own personal lives, and which of the two is given most prominence, is largely a matter of individual temperament and vocation; it is a question of what particular spiritual path we are individually called to follow.

If we are following the path of Eckhart, it should be obvious by now where our own priorities are going to lie. For him it is always the inner reality which is of paramount importance; it is what happens *within* that really counts. Yet the outer reality is not neglected, still less suppressed. In the formula 'going out while remaining within', it may well be that it is the 'remaining within' which is most fundamental. But there is no question of 'remaining within' totally and exclusively; there has to be a 'going out' as well. Perhaps it is the Silent Desert of Nameless Godhead, and the equally unfathomable and nameless Ground of the Soul, which draws the Eckhartian seeker most powerfully; but in the very act of plumbing

1. Luke 17:22.

these inner depths he will find himself 'melting out' and 'boiling' in loving communion with the Father, through the Son who is born in the soul through the Holy Spirit. Furthermore, he will find himself not merely 'boiling' but 'boiling over', impelled to creative and compassionate activity in the world, attempting to do something to relieve the suffering and blindness of his fellow-human beings. Looking at it another way, we can say that silence generates the Word, and the Word returns to silence. Silence has a certain priority, it precedes, underlies and follows the Word; it is what gives the Word depth and meaning. Yet the silence cannot remain forever unbroken; the Word has to be spoken out. There is a 'silent' conceiving of the Word within the Trinity as the Father speaks to the Son within his own depths; there is also an 'audible' speaking of the Word in the creation of the universe and in the Incarnation of the Redeemer. The same mystery of outer and inner, speech and silence, has to be re-enacted in our own lives. We cannot remain forever in the silent depths of the Soul's Ground, communing with the nameless transcendent; we also have to 'speak the Word', revealing to the world what we have understood of God through what we say, what we do, and by our whole manner of *being*. The glory of the Kingdom is both inner and outer; when the light of God has been kindled within us, we shall then find it outside us as well; God will, as Eckhart says, 'shine out' at us 'from all things'.

Let us suppose now that we have glimpsed something of this glory, or are at least on the way towards glimpsing it. Let us imagine that the mystical union, the Birth of God in the Soul, has occurred in us, or that we are at least moving towards it. What will our life then be like? What will be going on in our own inner depths, and what will our behaviour and attitude be like in our dealings with the outer world? Eckhart, following in the footsteps of the Arab philosopher, Avicenna, once said that the human soul has a double face: one is turned towards the world, where it is occupied with virtuous deeds; the other gazes directly upon God.[2] These are the two aspects of the Kingdom, the two directions in which we must look in order to see the glory of the face of God. Perhaps it would be

2. See Walshe, vol. 1, p. 231.

best to approach the inner one first, since according to
Eckhart's mind this is the more fundamental.

So far in this book we have not really faced the question
of 'spiritual practice', the question of prayer, meditation,
sacraments and worship. This is not an oversight on the
author's part; it is quite deliberate. One of the major purposes
of this book is to try to present Eckhart's teaching as a
balanced whole, taking care not to give any individual part
more stress than it ought to have in relation to the others.
To have treated extensively, at an early stage, the question
of prayer and 'spiritual exercises' would almost certainly have
led precisely to this kind of imbalance. Eckhart never wrote
a treatise on Prayer, and it is doubtful whether he would have
been interested in doing so. Why not? Because he is concerned
with teaching a spiritual way which encompasses the *whole* of
life, not merely its 'religious' or 'spiritual' parts. When people
start asking anxious questions about what sort of prayer or
'spiritual method' they should adopt, this often indicates a
split mentality, a tendency to separate off the 'religious' side
of life from the rest. Eckhart would not countenance this for
a moment. Real spiritual life is about loss of self, sacrifice,
inner transformation and change. It involves a radical alter-
ation of attitude which affects *every* element in our lives, even
the apparently most earthy and trivial. Now we are most of
us – perhaps all of us – very frightened at the prospect of this
kind of radical change and transformation of ourselves.
Rather than yield to it, throw ourselves into it, we do all we
can to fence it out, to keep it at bay. Meditation techniques
and 'methods of prayer' are sometimes a very subtle way of
doing this. Harassed business executives and bank managers
resort, in their spare time, to yoga and transcendental meditation. This provides them with periodic 'trips' which lack
the harmful side-effects of alcohol or drugs; it gets their
passions under control, eases nervous tension and reduces the
risk of ulcers. But does it necessarily lead to profound inner
change and transformation, loss of self, radical redirection of
life? Not in the least. All too often it simply increases the
power of ego, of self, by 'spiritualizing' it. After doing my
meditation practice, I 'feel' better, and more refreshed. I have
plugged in to the cosmic powerhouse and had my batteries
recharged. That enables me to return to my daily life and

activities *on exactly the same basis as before.* There has been no change, no sacrifice. I have given up nothing, save a little of my time. Refreshed now, by meditation, I can resume my habitual quest for money, power, influence, the manipulation and exploitation of other people. I have not really thrown away self. I have, in fact, strengthened it, given it more permanence by saturating it with incense smoke and permeating it with cosmic 'vibes'.

None of this is meant to be a criticism of meditation practices as such. The point is simply that by themselves they do not necessarily bring about any radical change in my personality or life. Exactly the same is true of more 'mainline' spiritual practices, like going to church and frequenting the sacraments. So long as these practices are fenced off within a little enclosure reserved for what I call my 'spiritual life', they are not going to have any very profound effect on my life as a whole. Until I try to let go of self and surrender to God in every moment of every day, my true spiritual life has not really started. We spent a lot of time in the preceding chapter thrashing out the question of whether Eckhart's way should be called 'mystical'. The answer is yes, we can call it that, provided we understand what true mysticism is. It is not supranormal experiences of ecstasy or rapture. It is union with God, brought about by total surrender of self. If I really want that, I do not have to do extraordinary things or go to far-away places in order to get it. I can have it now, provided I am prepared to surrender self and all things to God in perfect detachment, *and to keep on doing this constantly.*

In fact, however, I am not yet able to do this. I am held by various bonds of attachment which make my surrender only partial and qualified. If I want to learn detachment, I shall have to proceed by easy stages, surrendering one by one the things that hold me fettered.

Most people in twentieth-century Europe and America have a strong attachment to activity, haste, noise and talk. This is a very real obstacle to union with God, for two reasons. First, because it leads to dissipation and squandering of energy. Union with God is a transformation process in which colossal energy needs to be built up and intensified, as in processes of physical transformation. It is no accident that Eckhart likes to talk about 'melting' and 'boiling' and uses images drawn from alchemical techniques of transmutation. All this springs from his realization that radical inner change can only occur in conditions of great pressure, heat and accumulation of energy. This is the reason for his insistence on 'remaining within', enclosed, bent back upon one's inner life; because to do the opposite would disperse the energy and hinder the transformation. The second reason for severing my attachment to extraverted, hasty, talkative habits is because they build up the ego, the very illusion of self-permanence and self-importance which the spiritual life needs to dissolve. The more I talk, and the more I do, the more I feel that I *am* somebody, that I have a vital role to play in the world, that the world, in fact, will stop going round unless I am there to push it. This feeling is absurd, of course, but it is very deep and ingrained in all of us. To get rid of it we have to get rid of the activities which feed it.

That means the practice of at least some form of stillness, meditation and prayer. The ironical remarks made about these practices earlier in this book are not meant to imply that they have no value or importance; far from it. The irony was directed only against the idea that they are the *whole* of the spiritual life. They are not, they are only a part; but they are nevertheless an important part, and almost certainly, for twentieth-century people, an indispensable part. Detachment from creatures and images, withdrawal into the Soul's Ground, awareness of my own nothingness before God – none of this ought to be *restricted* to my hours of prayer and solitude; but it will almost certainly have to *start* there. It is perfectly true, as Eckhart says, that if a man has God truly within him, he will find him at all times and in all places. But the operative word here is 'if'. Most of us will find, in practice, that we shall be unable to find God amid noise and activity until we have first found him in inwardness and stillness.

When Eckhart exalts Martha above Mary, and makes fun of people who think God can only be found in solitary withdrawal, these remarks need to be taken in the context of the people he was probably talking to. He was talking, much of the time, to professional religious of his own Order, which, like the other Orders in the Middle Ages, had inherited a spirituality which was still largely monastic and ascetic. This meant there was a danger, for religious trained in this tradition, of overvaluing flight from the world and experiences of contemplative rapture. Detachment, for them, would therefore require that they should sacrifice some of their private ecstasy, and do something active to help the needy. But for us, in the twentieth century, the situation is the exact opposite. We are more likely to overvalue action and 'commitment', for the bias of our culture tends in this direction. Therefore detachment requires us to learn something of the 'monastic' values of silence, stillness and inwardness – unless these, too, become an attachment and hindrance which needs to be surrendered! Here again we are on the seesaw of paradox, and need to experience both sides of it in order to grasp it wholly.

Having decided, then, with some escape clauses, that prayer and meditation are going to have a certain importance in our lives, how are we going to set about them? Does Eckhart give us any clues on this? Yes, the clues are certainly there, provided we are prepared to extrapolate and interpret a little. Over and over again in his sermons he talks about withdrawing into the Soul's Ground, ridding the mind of external images and attachments, and directing the attention inwards. There is no harm in our interpreting this as instruction for prayer, provided we bear in mind that it is not meant to be exclusively that, as we saw in the preceding chapter. If we interpret the remarks in this way, then it is clear that Eckhart is recommending a practice of prayer similar to that which is called 'pure' prayer, which was taught in the Egyptian desert by Evagrius, later by some unknown Syrian monk under the name of Dionysius, and reappears in the fourteenth-century English treatise called *The Cloud of Unknowing*. People interested in this kind of prayer and anxious to practise it could do worse than read this particular treatise, which is short, clear, and exists in a number of good editions, including one in modern English. The general idea behind the treatise is Eckhartian enough: that God is an unfathomable, transcendent reality who cannot be fully expressed in any name, word, concept or picture in the mind, however traditional or sacrosanct. Therefore we are encouraged to look beyond such images and reach out in the darkness for that Mystery which we cannot conceive or understand. We cannot 'understand' God by means of our normal reasoning faculty, but we can *pine* for God, reach out to him, yearn for him who lies hidden in an impenetrable cloud of mystery. Blind motions of the will, a kind of inarticulate longing or craving, a 'dart of longing love' – this is the sort of prayer taught in *The Cloud*; and it is probably the best practice to help us get started on the Eckhartian way.

If, however, we combine Eckhart's teaching with the reading of *The Cloud* and the practice of its kind of prayer, we may find ourselves puzzled and perplexed by an apparent contradiction. Eckhart teaches a Way of Knowledge, as we have already seen, since he believes that it is through intellect, rather than will, that we become totally united with our goal. *The Cloud*, on the other hand, has a strongly anti-intellectual bias, or seems to have: it maintains that God can never be attained through knowing, but only through loving. The discrepancy here is more apparent than real. We need to remember that for Eckhart there are two kinds of knowing: a lower and a higher. The lower is what we might call the normal human faculty of discursive reasoning, which draws logical conclusions from sense data and images in the mind. This kind of knowing can never attain God: *The Cloud* is quite correct here, and Eckhart would agree entirely. But what Eckhart says, and *The Cloud* does not say, is that over and above this lower form of knowing there is a higher form which does not use images or logical reasoning but which unites immediately and intuitively with its object. The author of *The Cloud* seems not to have known about this higher intellect, writing as he was at a time when the old scholastic, and perhaps especially Dominican, teaching about it was being lost. Therefore what Eckhart considers as 'spiritual knowledge' is entirely consistent with prayer as taught in *The Cloud*; on the level of imagery, if not of theology, the two authors are at one. *The Cloud* speaks of a 'sparkle'; Eckhart speaks of a 'spark' – in German, *funkelin* – which is kindled in the Soul's Ground when union with God occurs. The imagery of fire, leaping up and striving heavenwards, is common to both. But Eckhart has a richer and subtler vocabulary and terminology for these deep matters, still having the old Dominican tradition to draw on, based on Aristotle, Plato and the Bible. For him love, at its purest, most intense and most quintessential, becomes *intellect*, which does not merely aspire to its goal like love, but unites with it. The fire and heat of love melt out into the pure, white light of intellect.

The 'knowledge' Eckhart talks about is thus not ordinary, mundane knowledge such as *The Cloud* despises. It includes what *The Cloud* would call 'love', but raises it to a degree where it is heightened, purified and intensified. The spirituality of Eckhart is not a guttering, smoky flame which crackles and splutters – it is more like a laser beam which cleaves whatever it falls upon, and penetrates it to the core.

Anyone who embarks upon the practice of imageless prayer will soon run up against the problem of distractions – irrelevant thoughts, wandering of the mind, memories of things undone, worries about things still to do. The advice of *The Cloud* corresponds exactly with Eckhart's on this point. Both warn us against trying to eliminate these distractions by any kind of forceful act of will. That leads only to strain and exhaustion, and takes us nowhere. *The Cloud* says that when faced with distractions we should 'glance over their shoulder', not try to thrust them aside but look beyond them, always insisting, however gently – not this, not this. Eckhart takes a very similar line. Asking the question, how can I be the sort of man who is 'void of alien images, as empty as he was when he did not exist', he answers that even if my mind were full of all the images which human beings can conceive, provided I am not *attached* to them, so long as I do not cling to them or identify with them, 'then in truth I would be a virgin, untrammelled by any images, just as I was when I was not'.[3] Though Eckhart is almost certainly not talking exclusively about prayer here, none the less what he says applies to it and represents what his counsel would surely be on the matter.

It is easy to see from all this that Eckhart's teaching on prayer, and on the kind of spiritual life that flows out from prayer, has a double aspect: positive and negative. The negative attitude is that of detachment: when images and distractions, memories of the past and anticipations of the future arise in the mind, we are to *detach* from them – not too forcefully or violently, but firmly and resolutely. This leads to the state of mind which Eckhart describes as 'virginal' – a

3. Walshe, vol. 1, p. 71.

state in which the mind is clear, light, free and unencumbered
by its contents, whatever these may be. Such a state is already
a high degree of union with God, though not the highest; it
is a passive, receptive state in which the soul, detached from
self and creatures, is able to receive God into its depths. It is
not enough, however, by itself. The negative, receptive attitude of detachment has to be complemented by another which
is more positive, fiery and active. This means a constant,
deliberate and unwavering desire and questing for the
unknown, unnameable God. It is the 'dart of longing love'
which *The Cloud* speaks of: in Eckhart's own terminology it is
the 'spark' which leaps heavenwards and will be satisfied
with nothing less than the ultimate truth and reality. Once
this 'spark' is kindled in me, I am no longer merely a *virgin*,
I am also a *wife*. Not only do I *receive* God into myself,
passively; I *give birth to him*, actively. This is a deeper union
with God. It is the Birth of God in the Soul's Ground, which
is the aim and goal of all Eckhart's teaching.

To be virginal and detached, wifely and kindled with fire,
will begin in our periods of inner withdrawal and imageless
prayer, and once learned there, will overflow into all other
areas of our life – provided we let it, and are prepared to
make the ncessary sacrifices to ensure its happening. The two
aspects of the spiritual life – virginal detachment and wifely
kindling of the spark – are described in the context of life as
a whole in the very deep and practical *Talks of Instruction*,
which are in many ways the best introduction to Eckhart's
thought for people who are still new to it. In chapter vii he
describes the virginal state as one in which we are not
'impeded' by the things that surround us, and no 'lasting
image' remains in us. In other words, whatever the circumstances may be in which we find ourselves, we will not be
dominated or swallowed up by them so that we forget God:
we will not become drunk on joy or depressed by sorrow, but
will look beyond all these essentially changing and impermanent circumstances to the unchanging God who underlies
them. Especially we will not be dominated by the memories of
the past. Whatever experiences we have recently undergone,
however powerfully they may have moved us, will not over-
whelm us *now* or qualify our total freedom, lightness and
readiness to respond to the Will of God as it presents itself

to us in the present moment. But Eckhart insists that all this, good and necessary though it may be, 'should not suffice for us'. It is not enough simply to be virginal, detached from circumstances; we also have to be 'wifely', and actively, even passionately, seek God in them. We have to treat each moment as an Apocalypse, in which God is likely to return to earth at any moment, so we have to be vigilant and watchful, in case we are caught napping and miss his arrival. This is not an attitude of virginal purity and detachment but of active striving. As Eckhart says: 'This requires diligence and we must be prepared to give everything that one can contribute in mind and strength', unlike the attitude of detachment which he seems to think relatively easy to acquire after a little practice.

We have seen how this double life, as virgin and wife, starts in our periods of withdrawal and imageless prayer. This will lead to our perception of the glory of the Kingdom in our inner life. But how shall we come to see that same glory in the relatively external areas of our life: liturgical and communal prayer, sacraments, life in the Church and in the world at large? How will it affect our life in society, our sense of being involved in history, in sowing the seeds of the future in the soil of the present moment? I shall end this chapter with a brief consideration of these questions.

First, there is the question of our liturgical and sacramental life. On this point Eckhart has often been sadly misunderstood. Many people, writing and talking about him, seem to have got hold of the idea that he is teaching some form of 'transcendental meditation' – an introverted withdrawal into the depths of oneself that makes church worship, doctrine and sacraments superfluous. This is a very grave mistake. Whatever Eckhart says to us is based on the assumption that we are already practising Christians, faithful to the Church's teaching and nourished by the Church's sacraments. He does not dwell on this much in his sermons, for the simple reason that he takes it for granted. After all, a sermon is preached in a church, and the people who have come to hear it will be, for the most part, believers who, after hearing the sermon, will very probably proceed to make their communion. Furthermore, the medieval Germany in which Eckhart lived was not a secular or pluralist society: life was infiltrated by

the Church's influence on practically every level, so much
could be taken for granted then which could not be now.
Lastly, anyone who seriously doubts the importance which
Eckhart attributed to Church and sacraments should read
the more didactic and theological sermons in volume 4 of the
Latin Works (where he expounds the theology of the sacraments fairly fully) and also the *Talks of Instruction*, where he
stresses the need for frequent confession, communion, and
obedience to ecclesiastical superiors. His own fidelity to these
things is attested by what we know of his life. There is no
evidence to suggest that he was lax in the saying of his daily
Office and Mass; and his loyalty to the Pope was made clear
by his behaviour during the trial and afterwards.

If we really want to get this question of Church and sacraments into proper perspective, we need to see it in the context
of his general teaching about the Outer and the Inner Man;
about 'going out' yet 'remaining within'. It is perfectly true
that the Inner Man always has the priority for Eckhart. But
the Inner Man is not the Whole Man; the Outer Man exists,
too, and has his rights and needs. It is fairly clear that Eckhart
sees the sacraments as being mainly concerned with the
healing and purification of the Outer Man. He is not being
supercilious or derogatory here. He merely means that the
sacraments will not affect our inner life very much unless we
have the right inner disposition towards them. It is characteristic of him always to stress the inner disposition, saying, for
instance, in the *Talks of Instruction*, that it is a holier thing to
tread on a stone when well-disposed than to go to communion
when ill-disposed. That is typical Eckhartian shock-language,
to jolt us into sharper awareness. It does not mean that going
to communion is superfluous or inessential. The very same
Talks of Instruction in which these remarks occur also discuss
at some length the usefulness of scrupulous confession and
proper preparation for communion. What he does mean is
that outward actions, even of the holiest kind, have only a
relative value: they are meant to bring the Outer Man into
line with the Inner Man, and it is the Inner Man, in the last
analysis, who counts. When all is said and done, our final
destination is heaven, where there are no Masses or queues
for confession.

If, then, we are following the Eckhartian path ourselves,

we should not think we can do it simply by means of imageless prayer and detachment towards worldly activities. It is a Christian way which we are pursuing, grounded upon the Incarnation, so we need the Church with its doctrines, guidance and sacraments, since these perpetuate certain aspects of Jesus' life among us today. For our day-to-day spiritual life, it is obvious that the most important are confession and communion, for these are our regular nourishment, as opposed to sacraments such as baptism or confirmation, which come into play only at specific points in our development. It is easy to see, too, how confession and communion relate to the two aspects of our inner life – the virginal and the wifely – which we were looking at earlier. Penance and reconciliation relate to detachment, whereby we let go of that attachment to self and creatures which is the source of sin; the Eucharist relates to fiery union with God and transformation into his likeness, even into oneness with him. The *Talks of Instruction* have a lot to say about a detached, free attitude towards experience and life in the world, so it is natural that they should also treat fairly fully of the sacrament of penance. The *Sermons*, on the other hand, are very concerned with mystical union and the Birth of God in the Ground of the Soul; so it is not surprising to find this awesome mystery of transformation discussed in connection with the Eucharist in a sermon for Maundy Thursday.[4]

In this sermon two points are made which, if we group them and put them into practice, will greatly help our practice of prayer – both our private, imageless prayer and our more verbal and symbolic prayer as part of the worshipping Church. The first is to remember that the ultimate goal of our striving is the transcendent nameless God, who cannot be fully expressed in any created image. So even very holy prayers and actions, such as we carry out in the Church's liturgy, are not ends but means; they point beyond what is revealed to that which remains forever unrevealed; they point beyond words to the everlasting silence from which all words come and to which they must all return. It is possible for us, weak human beings as we are, to become very 'churchy' in a bad sense, getting very wrapped up in details of ceremonial

4. See Walshe, vol. 1, pp. 235 and 241.

and church furnishings as though these had absolute value –
as though they were God himself. If we let ourselves do this,
we have strayed from the path. It is a great error to let our
longing for God be eclipsed by our interest in the *things* of
God. So even in our verbal prayers and liturgical worship we
should still be reaching out into the darkness, seeking to
pierce the symbol, to penetrate the veil.

The second point which Eckhart makes in this Maundy
Thursday sermon is deeper and more mysterious, and will
touch our prayer life in its most intimate part. Eckhart is
speaking of the mystery of transformation, and how it is
effected both in the sacred species – the bread and wine which
become the Body and Blood of Christ – and in the human
soul, which becomes God himself in the mystical union. Many
people have been shocked at Eckhart's language here; at his
insistence that in the Birth of God in the Soul we are not
merely *united* with God, but actually *become* God. But it is
important for us to understand that this identity with God
occurs only *to the extent that* (in Eckhart's Latin, *inquantum*) we
let go of self and creatures. Once we become nothing, then
we are filled with God's infinite being. In the 'eating'
symbolism of the Eucharist, this means that we do not transform God into ourselves, as we transform the ordinary food
we eat into ourselves. On the contrary, it is God who transforms us into himself. We may seem, outwardly, to be taking
a meal; but in fact, inwardly, we are becoming food for
God. The Eucharist, and the mystical union, are not really
something that we do, but something that God does.

Perhaps our prayer starts to become really deep and meaningful once we begin to realize and experience this fact. It is
not we who pray, but Christ who prays in us. We do not
know what to desire or to strive for, but as St Paul tells us
in the Epistle to the Corinthians, the Spirit intercedes for us
and plumbs the depths of God. The Word which made the
Universe and redeemed us as Jesus of Nazareth, is continually
resounding within us and drawing us into the mystery of the
Trinity and the unfathomable Godhead, the Silent Desert.
Rather than try to *make* this happen, we should simply *let* it
happen. We do not eat; we are eaten. We do not pray; we
are prayed. Our prayer is like a bell-note which wells up from
the depths below consciousness and dies away in the heights

beyond consciousness. It is a wave on which we are carried; and all we have to do is to let it take us where it wills. That prayer can hardly be refused which is prayed by God himself.

And what of the outward, more communal aspect of our life in Church and in society as a whole? Does the Way of Eckhart really include this dimension of things and make sufficient provision for it?

Some modern Christians, on reading Eckhart, get the impression of a spirituality which may be very deep but is also intensely private and individualistic. In an age like our own, when we feel an increasing need to belong to a community, and to sense our solidarity with other human beings, we may feel that Eckhart has nothing very much to say to us. But this would be a very hasty and superficial judgement. If we try to stand back a little and take a more balanced view of the present situation, we shall see that the communal pole of the spiritual life, important though it is, needs to be complemented by the exploration of the individual soul and its inner depths. The current popularity of Eastern meditation teaching makes it clear that this need is a real one and very keenly felt by a large number of people. In this field Eckhart is obviously a specialist, and we can surely excuse him for concentrating on it most of the time, and not blame him for failing to talk about international peace and justice, or the problems of the Third World.

More importantly, however, Eckhart poses a challenge to our ideas of 'community' and 'solidarity'. If we are really able to grasp what he is saying, we shall find ourselves forced to reconsider what exactly a healthy and authentic 'living with and for others' might mean. Does it mean an inability to be alone, a constant and compulsive throwing of oneself into social life and activity? Hardly. No person can live properly with others unless he has also learned to live with himself. If I plunge into social activity in order to escape from my own unresolved inner tensions, there is no virtue in that; and, what is more, I am more likely to do harm to others than good. Even though the enterprises and causes I engage in may be good in themselves, if my motives for doing them are unsound, they are almost certain to turn out badly in the long run. Only that activity which is done from the Ground of the Soul, in perfect detachment and renunciation of self,

will have truly lasting and positive effects, because it is then
not done by me but by God, and is permeated by his wisdom
and power. The activity in itself may be inconspicuous and
seemingly trivial, but its long-term effects will be colossal, as
is bound to be the case if God is the true agent. So if we want
to be good and useful members of society it is very important
that we enter the depths of ourselves, discover God in the
Soul's Ground, and learn to act from that centre. It is in the
mystery of the Silent Desert, the Nameless Godhead, that
the Persons of the Trinity find their Ground of Unity, and
are thus able to 'melt' and 'boil' into communion with each
other. Similarly, it is by entering our own Silent Desert, the
inviolable and nameless Ground of the Soul, that we are able
to 'melt' and 'boil' in creative and loving relationships with
each other. This is bound to be so, since it is in this Ground
that we discover the 'universal human nature' which is
common to us all, whatever our character, race, class, or
religion. It is the Ground, or basis, for human solidarity as
the Godhead is the Ground, or basis, for the communion of
Persons within the Trinity.

If any order is to be brought into the chaos of the modern
world, if anything is to be salvaged from the wreckage and
made the foundation of a better world in the future, this
can only be done by those who have attained what Eckhart
attained – loss of self and surrender to God in the Soul's
Ground. It is that, and that alone, which can produce real
change, because in the last analysis the world can only be
changed by changing the people who live in it. If we try to
work exclusively on the external level, on the plane of action,
our change will be merely cosmetic, and fundamentally
nothing will have altered.

So we cannot claim that Eckhart has nothing to say to us
about how to cope with our urgent communal, social and
political problems. It is obviously no use our asking him for
any *detailed programme* for dealing with specific issues. His
medieval context and particular field of interest rule out any
possibility of his providing us with that kind of help. What
we can ask from him, however, and what he can certainly
give us, is the fundamental *formula* for tackling problems of
this nature. It is simply this: if you want to change the world,
change yourself. If you want to gain the world, let it go, and

surrender to God. If you want to find God in the world, seek him first in yourself. Once you have surrendered to God in the Soul's Ground, and entered the inner kingdom, then the outer kingdom will also be opened to you. But you must not surrender to God *in order* to gain the world! That would be acting from selfish motives; it would not be action 'without why'; it would not be true renunciation. We can only gain what we have truly let go; there lies the paradox.

The same formula is valid for the 'apocalyptic' questions which trouble us as we witness the death of an old culture and watch for the precursory signs of a new. It is not the attitude of a truly wise and enlightened person – one in whom the spiritual intellect is fully awake – to become obsessed with the currents of history and how to channel them or direct them. Eckhart himself refused to get entangled in such questions, though he could have done so if he had wished. Almost a century before him, the visionary abbot Joachim of Flora had speculated daringly about the great rhythms and phases of history, prophesying the advent of a New Age of the Spirit, in which the traditional forms and structures of religion would be superseded. Eckhart might have seen himself as the inaugurator of this New Age – especially since Joachim had calculated that it would begin in 1260, roughly the date of Eckhart's own birth! But nowhere in Eckhart's writings can we find any trace of interest in the current of millenarian speculation which Joachim had triggered off. 'The fullness of time', says Eckhart in a sermon on the Annunciation, 'is where there is no more time.' Our task is to concentrate on the present moment and on its demands, because it is here, and here alone, that time intersects with eternity. The aim is to become detached from time and space, and to cast them into the eternity of God. In doing this we are actually fulfilling the purpose of the Incarnation; for God did not become Man so as to enslave us to history, but to free us from it. The great cycles of time, and the great phases of transition between one epoch and the next, will unfold as they are meant to, provided we surrender our possessive grasp of them and leave God free to act through us.

If we make a serious practice of the Eckhartian way, and begin, however dimly at first, to glimpse its goal, we shall sense a fundamental change in our attitude to another

problem which preoccupies us a great deal at this present
time, which is the problem of *freedom*. Today we tend to see
freedom primarily in social and political terms, and indeed
that aspect of it is extremely urgent and important. But
Eckhart, nevertheless, would almost certainly take the view
that *inner* freedom is more fundamental, and much harder to
achieve – mainly because most of us imagine we have it
already. Down the centuries there has been much debate
among philosophers and theologians as to whether human
beings have 'free will' or not. Yet the truth of the matter –
not always grasped, by any means – is that free will is not
something we possess automatically, like having two arms or
two legs. It is something we have to work at, something we
have to earn. In most of us, most of the time, it exists only
as a potential, not often realized in concrete fact. I go about
my daily occupations, working, talking, eating, sleeping,
imagining that I *choose* to do all these things, that I 'will'
them. As a rule, however, I do nothing of the sort. Most of
these so-called 'actions' of mine are in fact *reactions*,
conditioned by my physical and mental makeup, my past
history, by the social and cultural environment in which I
have grown up, and by the various stimuli, pleasant or otherwise, which I may be experiencing at the present moment.
This so-called 'action' of mine, which I think is freely willed,
is in fact mostly habitual and automatic; I am a robot, simply
functioning according to the programming and conditioning
I have received. The moment we start to gain any degree of
true self-knowledge, we shall be astonished and horrified at
how much of what we consider our 'own' life, thoughts and
feelings, is mere robot-like reaction to conditioning. This is
true also of our inner, personal life: the sort of people we like
or dislike, the sort of religious and political views we have,
the sort of things we like to eat, the sort of recreation we like
to take, and so on. Prejudice and hatred, whether of race,
religion, or class, such as is tearing the modern world apart,
is largely a matter of passive reaction to conditioning; a truly
'free man' is not governed by these things. And we cannot
hope to abolish social and political strife so long as we remain
passive to the influences which provoke it, so long as we
remain slaves to our conditioning.

Eckhart talks quite a lot about being free – *frei*, in German.

Another word he uses for the same thing is *ledig* – light, untrammelled, unbound. It is a state which is not exactly 'given', but which can be attained if we strive for it. That means effort and sacrifice. It is possible to attain it, for two reasons. The first is that God himself wants us to have it, and will certainly give the grace to anyone who is sincerely striving for it. The second is the nature of the human soul itself, which in its Ground or innermost essence is free from time and space, and even from personality: 'It is ineffable, as he (God) is ineffable'; it has no name. That means it is free and exempt from external conditioning; it is 'above all that'; it is noble, or *edel*, to use Eckhart's own word: that is, it is naturally subject only to God, not to any created thing. The reason why, in our actual daily lives, we do not realize this freedom, but remain enslaved to conditioning factors which are by their own nature 'beneath us', is because we are unaware of the existence of this Ground, and of how to get into it and act from within it. Once we do enter the Ground of the Soul, and unite there with the Ground of God, then, and only then, is real freedom attained. It is a freedom all the truer and more valuable in that it remains unaffected by external conditions, however adverse. We may find ourselves, for example, in an unjust and repressive society, in which our basic social and political rights are denied us. Yet, though outwardly enslaved, a man who is united with God in the Soul's Ground remains inwardly free; and the *mere existence* in the world of people like that ensures that in the end right must prevail, even on the external, observable level.

There is no need to say any more now on *how* we are to get into the Soul's Ground, renounce self and creatures, and become one with God; we have gone into this already. It is done by becoming 'virgin' and 'wife', by coupling detachment from impermanent external conditions with fiery striving after the eternal, transcendent God, in every moment of our lives, whatever we may be thinking or doing. Before we end this chapter, however, there is one further thing we need to look at briefly, because it is important, very much a part of real life as actually lived, and something we have not really touched on earlier in this book. It is the question of suffering, and the encounter with evil.

No one reading Eckhart could accuse him of having a

morbid obsession with suffering. The prevailing impression
he gives is one of lightness, radiance and joy. Devotional
meditation on the physical and mental torments of Christ's
Passion – bleeding wounds, crown of thorns, contorted body,
and so on – was extremely popular in his day, and practised
even by certain of his own followers, such as Suso and Tauler;
but he himself does not advocate it or show any interest in
it. Yet he knows about suffering; he sees that it is an intrinsic
part of life as we have to live it at present; no one can enter
the Soul's Ground or attain union with God without passing
through this dark gate. He considered it important enough
to dedicate an entire book to it: *The Book of Spiritual Comfort*,
written to console Queen Agnes of Hungary in the many
misfortunes which had befallen her. Yet even here, his
perspective remains very much his own, as is revealed by the
title. His aim is to provide *comfort* and *consolation* – in German,
tröstung – for the suffering Queen, and others like her. There
is no suggestion that suffering has any kind of intrinsic value,
that it is in any way an end in itself. It is simply a fact of
life, something which we must inevitably encounter on the
way to God. Therefore, rather than dwell on it or become
obsessed with it, Eckhart tries to show us how to cope with
it and overcome it.

The first thing we have to do is to recognize that it is
necessary and inevitable. As a rule, we make it worse by
failing to recognize it, by refusing to accept it, by constantly
running away from it, because it seems to us a meaningless,
cruel, unjust imposition. I say to myself: 'Why should I have
to go through this ghastly business? I may be a rather unim-
pressive character in many ways; maybe I do some rather
bad things from time to time; but nothing so bad as to deserve
this. If God is wise, and just, and loving, why doesn't he
simply forgive and let me off?' This is the complaint of Job,
the anguished human cry of protest against the *meaninglessness*
and *injustice* of suffering. But the truth of the matter is that it
is not meaningless or unjust, and it immediately becomes
easier to bear once we realize this. The author of the Book of
Job has reached this insight, and so has Eckhart; and both
of them make the same comment: our load of suffering will
be lightened the moment we accept it and stop fighting it,

the moment we understand that it is not an injustice on God's part but springs inevitably from the nature of things.

As we saw earlier, all the suffering and evil in the world springs from the fact that it is not God. God *is*, absolutely; he is infinite, unconditioned Being. In him there is no 'not', no negation; he is, as Eckhart likes to say in his Latin works, *negatio negationis*, the negation of negation. He is utterly and unconditionally positive. But we, and the universe we live in, are not like that. We are not infinite, absolute being; there is an element in us of non-being, of nothingness, of negation, of *not*. That is the source of all our suffering. In our ordinary, unredeemed state in this world, there is no escape from suffering. It is no use fleeing from it, trying to shut it out by clinging to material securities and comforts; for these, too, have their own admixture of *not*. That means that we are liable to lose them at any time; they can be taken from us by sickness or some other reversal of fortune; even if we keep them they are liable to go stale on us and fail to satisfy us any more. And in the end comes death, which takes everything away, whether good or ill. So there is nothing in this world which we can cling to in order to shut out suffering or cure it. The very clinging is itself a form of suffering, a reaction of panic before the emptiness and nothingness we sense at the heart of ourselves. It is, in fact, the worst kind of suffering, because *it leads nowhere.* It does not make us stronger or wiser; it does not loosen our bonds but merely draws them tighter.

There is only one way to overcome suffering, and that is to unite with God. By detachment from self and creatures, we get rid of *not*, and there is nothing then which can touch us. Having thrown away our own creatureliness and emptiness, we are filled with God's divinity and fullness. Now the very process of learning this detachment also brings suffering; but it differs from merely selfish, worldly suffering in that it is *meaningful*, it is leading us somewhere, and thus becomes easier to bear. Gaining detachment is bound to be painful at first, because it involves letting go of things which we have come to depend on and think essential to our life. We may accept in theory that God is all, and creatures are nothing, but in practice we do not feel that this is so, or live as if it were so. To really learn this truth involves renunciation, and renunciation is inevitably painful. But we can bear it once we realize that it is breaking our bonds, leading us to God, and enabling us to live free, creative lives which will bring real good to the world.

Therefore there are two kinds of suffering: there is one which springs from selfish clinging to creatures, and another which springs from the attempt to detach from creatures and cling to God. But the two kinds are very different. The first binds, the second liberates. The first crushes, and is hard to bear; the second strengthens and is even, in a strange, paradoxical sense, easy to bear. The fact that the second sort is easier is not only because we accept its necessity and see that it is leading us to freedom. It is also because God himself steps in and helps us to carry it, even, in effect, carries it for us. That is why very holy people can endure the most appalling torments and privations, which would crush a lesser person: it is because they are not carrying the burden alone; God is in them, carrying it for them. This explains the heroism of the martyrs, and also, of course, the endurance of Christ on Calvary. Once we accept suffering as coming from God, and reach out to God in it and through it, then God comes into it and shares it with us. As Eckhart says, very strikingly, in the *Talks of Instruction*: whatever we suffer for God's sake, God himself suffers first. God becomes like a garment clothing us, so that anything which touches us touches him first. Therefore, when it reaches us, its character has changed, through the fact that it has passed through God, and has become impregnated, so to speak, with his flavour.

That is how we can know whether the suffering we endure comes from sin – attachment to self and creatures; or from God – detachment from self and creatures and striving for union. Selfish suffering is hard, unselfish suffering is easier and even a kind of joy. There is nothing masochistic or morbid about this 'joy'. It is not rejoicing in suffering for its own sake, or thinking that suffering has some kind of intrinsic value. It is accepting, realistically, the inevitability of suffering in the process of learning detachment, and rejoicing in the increased communion with God which comes to us in the heart of suffering. This ability to rejoice with God in the heart of suffering is, in Eckhart's view, the highest kind of virtue. To endure pain for God's sake is good, but to be able to rejoice in the midst of the pain is better. It is, in fact, not merely better, but the best.

This, then, is the road we must take if we wish to see the Glory of the Kingdom, both without and within: detachment and fiery striving. It leads to true joy, true freedom, and victory over suffering. It brings us into union with God, and makes us able to become an influence for real good in the world. No other road will do that. The option is clear; it is for us to make our choice.

9   Echoes

It is time now for us to look back over the path we have travelled in this book, and try to take in Eckhart's teaching as a whole. Then we can assess the degree of importance it has for us, and the extent to which we may find it useful as we attempt to live our own spiritual lives in the present-day world.

We might sum up the path of Eckhart by saying that it has two aspects: one of *movement*, and one of *repose*. On the one hand there is development, growth, process, change and transformation. There is energy, too, and dynamism. On the other hand there is stillness, a sense of eternity, and of conditions which are not subject to change or transformation but remain everlastingly the same. Nothing is gained here, and nothing is lost; all is held continually in balance. The first aspect, that of movement, has a kind of story to it; it is an epic, a heroic narrative. It is the *history* of God's dealings with the world, how the world has flowed forth from God, and how it must ultimately flow back again to its source. It shows how the seeds of this process lie within God himself, as the Divine Persons emerge from the Nameless Godhead, commune, and return to the Godhead through their total unity with each other. It shows how the Father, in uttering forth the Son, also utters forth the universe, yet at the same time calls the universe back into himself, through the Incarnation and redemptive work of Christ, and through the 'mystical' Birth of the Son in the Ground of the Soul. For this is what the Birth in the Soul's Ground is really all about: it is creation returning to its Creator. This is the purpose of our human life on earth: to be the means or medium by which that which comes forth from God can return to God. We are not meant to live either disembodied, purely spiritual lives, like the angels, or purely physical and sensual lives, like animals and plants; we are meant to inhabit both worlds, both 'lower' and 'higher', and maintain the flow of energy between them. When I emerge from a state of inner withdrawal and abandonment to God in prayer, and take up my duties in the everyday world, I am establishing a flow of energy whereby the light, life, wisdom and power of Heaven enter our world to enliven and transform it. When I turn away from everyday preoccupations to commune with God in prayer, losing myself and all creatures in him, the everyday world, which is part of me, becomes an offering and sacrifice made to God; it is changed and transformed by being returned to its Source; there is a flow of energy from earth back into Heaven. This movement, from Heaven to earth and back again, is continual; it is happening during every moment of every day. It is also rhythmical and natural, a movement of expansion and contraction, of breathing in and breathing out; the whole of spiritual life, seen in this way, appears as the beating of a great heart.

The second aspect of Eckhart's path, the aspect of repose, concerns the relationship between God and creatures, which remains fundamentally the same despite the various processes of change and transformation which the creatures undergo. This relationship preoccupied Eckhart as a theologian and a philosopher rather than as a teacher of spiritual living in the everyday world; it is the relationship between Being and Nothingness. God alone has being in the truest and fullest sense; creatures have it only in a partial or conditional sense. From the point of view of God, then, you and I, and all creatures, are *nothing* – we do not possess being truly as God possesses it. Nevertheless, the fleeting, loaned-out kind of being we have is the only sort we really know and understand, so from our point of view it is God who is 'nothing', since he is utterly beyond what we call 'being'. That is why Eckhart will sometimes use the term 'nothing' to refer to God, and at other times to refer to creatures, depending on the point of view he is adopting at the time. This might seem to set up an unbridgeable gulf between God and creatures – between God and me. I can never have 'being' in God's sense; I can never become fully one with him. But in fact the gulf between God and us is not quite so unbridgeable as that. The being we have is God's own being, even though we have it in a different way from him; it is something he and we *share*. Also, our share in it can be *increased*, to the point at which the distinction between me, and God, though never obliterated, nevertheless becomes imperceptible. This is the work of the Incarnate and Redemptive Word, born historically in Bethlehem and mystically in the Soul's Ground. So here we have a set of conditions which are always the same and never change: God is God, and creature is creature. Yet God and creature share something, and continue to do so, so long as the creature exists at all.

These two aspects of movement and repose represent the two sides of Eckhart's life and work. The first preoccupied him as a spiritual teacher, guiding human individuals to union with God in their own lives. The second preoccupied him as a theologian, and as an expert in philosophy and metaphysics. The first led him to write the daring and gripping German sermons which compel and fascinate, even today. The second led him to write the compendious Latin works, in which depth of speculation is matched by extraordinary clarity in expression and presentation. In both, however, the element of *paradox* is paramount, which is why we should see it as the key to his path. Paradox is present in the process of movement, because although all things do flow forth from God and back again, the flowing and returning are continual and simultaneous, so that in a sense everything is always both 'outside' and 'inside', as in the formula 'going out yet remaining within', which we looked at earlier. Paradox is also present in the metaphysical relationship between God and Creature, because both are in a sense 'being' and both are, in another sense, 'nothing'. What is more, the gulf between Creator and creatures is paradoxical, because it both can, and cannot, be bridged. God becomes a creature, in the Incarnation, yet remains God; in the Birth of God in the Soul's Ground, the creature becomes God, yet remains a creature. We may well quote Eckhart's own ironical phrase here, and say that 'whoever understands this has been preached to enough'.

As a practical guide for souls, Eckhart taught the dynamic movement of outflow and 'back-flow'; as a scholar and metaphysician he taught the dialectic of Being and Nothingness;

yet these, too, cannot really be separated, for they go together always in his thought, and furthermore relate to each other paradoxically. There are not two Eckharts, one practical and the other theoretical; neither are there two Eckhartian paths, one for everyday life and the other for intellectual speculation; there is only one Eckhart and one Eckhartian path, in which theory and practice are inseparable. We can distinguish them for the sake of analysis, but to do this too radically would lead to falsification, for, as Wordsworth said: 'We murder to dissect.' What brings the two together is the Higher Intellect, the Eye of the Heart, which we looked at earlier in this book. Spiritual Intellect, as Eckhart understands and teaches it, is highly paradoxical. There can be no doubt that the way which he is inviting us to follow is a way of *knowledge*; it springs from an ability to *see* things as they really are, without veils or distortions – God, ourselves, and the union between the two. But this 'knowledge' is not something pale, abstract and bloodless; it is something *lived*, with fire, intensity and passion. Cool detachment and fiery longing – these must always go together and be *experienced* together as a single reality; this is the only way to grasp the truth of God. The very language which Eckhart uses to describe mystical union shows this double character of the spiritual goal. Sometimes he talks about the Father 'speaking' the Son in the Ground of the Soul; this is the language of detached intellectuality, the language of knowledge and vision. But at other times he talks about the 'birth' of the Son in the Ground of the Soul; and that is a warmer, more human language, hinting even at the 'motherhood' of God, which Julian of Norwich said so much about. Until heart and head, intellect and love, are one in us, we have not really grasped the reality of God, nor really embarked on the path of Eckhart.

This is probably why his way, though entirely right for some, is not right for all. It can only be right for those whose spiritual longing is for knowledge and vision. Wanting to 'know' in this sense certainly does not mean being an 'intellectual' in the sense of being erudite, scholarly and academic; but it does mean wanting above all to see the *truth* about things, wanting to see what *is* rather than what we would like, even though the two are not, in the last analysis, contradictory.

Nevertheless there are certain elements in Eckhart's message which are surely valuable for anyone attempting to live a serious spiritual life, even though they may not find themselves able to follow his whole teaching. No one who listens to Eckhart attentively can fail to perceive certain resonances, certain 'echoes', as the title of this chapter calls them – certain implications for the present and future, certain fruitful paths as yet hardly explored. So perhaps it would be useful to glance at a few of these briefly, and with this bring the present book to its close.

The great merit and value of Eckhart's vision, it seems to me, is its *transparency* and *radiance*. It lets in the light, instead of shutting it out or tingeing it with a particular colour. This could be of immense value for a world in which the traditional religious forms have become rather 'opaque'. What does this mean? It means that Christianity, although relatively new on the historical scene when compared to the ancient religions of Asia, is nevertheless an old religion now: the dazzling intuitive insights of its first beginnings have found expression in highly developed forms of theology, liturgy and church hierarchy, which, precisely because they *are* so highly developed, precisely because human beings have put so much into them, can seem to be entirely satisfying and valid on the human level alone. The sense of the transcendent mystery of God, the unknowable, the unnameable, can get lost. What ought to be a window, opening up onto the light of Heaven, can become a coloured pane, giving it a certain hue, or even a curtain, shutting it out altogether. Perhaps what is wrong with our modern religion is not so much the forms themselves in which it finds expression, but rather the kind of *value* which we have come to give those forms, a value which is too absolute. Theology, liturgy, church hierarchy and pastoral works – these are ultimately only means and instruments; they are not God himself; they are not the ultimate goal of our striving; and they exert a deadening effect the moment we start to consider them as ultimate. That does not mean that we should cast them aside. It means that we need to learn to look through them; to remember that they are means, not ends; to keep our eyes fixed on the transcendent Goal. This is what Eckhart is continually encouraging us to do; it is the whole thrust of his teaching. He is no iconoclast or revolutionary in the sense of wanting to overthrow the existing church order; but he wants us to regard that order for what it truly is: a framework within which to seek union with the transcendent God. This is real religious radicalism, in the sense of returning to the *radix* or root. It is also real religious renewal, for renewal comes about, as the Second Vatican Council reminded us, by 'returning to the sources'. These 'sources', in the last analysis, are not New Testament texts or biblical blueprints for church and community life, however valuable these may be; the real sources are in God and in the human heart. It is there that Eckhart invites us to look: in the Silent Desert of Nameless Godhead, from which the Divine Persons well up like inexhaustible springs; in the Ground of the Soul, where God is born in us and we are born in God. If we find this, we shall have found what religion is supposed to be all about, and our spiritual life is bound to be revitalized, even in the social and communal aspects which so preoccupy us today.

Another great service Eckhart can render us is to restore our sense of the spiritual life as a *search* or *quest*. Precisely because God is transcendent, and in this life we can never lay hold of him definitively, we can never say that we have 'found', that we have 'arrived', that we now 'know what it is all about'. Perhaps very few of us do say these things, or even think them consciously; but we certainly think them unconsciously and act as though they were true. The way of Eckhart, however, like any authentic spiritual way, is one of continual searching. Even the great spiritual event which he talks about – the Birth of God in the Soul's Ground – has nothing final or definitive about it. It is not an end, but a beginning. Once it happens, we cannot say that we have 'arrived'; but we can say that at long last we have truly 'started'. That means we must go further. After God is born in us, there has to follow the even more mysterious process whereby we 'bear the Son back into the Father'. That is a lifelong process, and reaches its fulfilment only beyond the grave. Meanwhile we must continue on the path of gentle detachment and fiery striving. There always remains something more to be given up, some new depth of God to be sounded, some deeper understanding of ourselves and the world.

Lastly, we shall reap great benefit if we allow ourselves to be influenced and affected by Eckhart's immense *openness*. As one who had some sense and experience of ultimate Truth, he knew how to respect truth in all its different modes of expression, however strange or alien some of them might appear at first. He drew not only from the Bible and from Christian authors, but also from pagan, Jewish and Arab sources. For him the truth was always the truth, and any glimpse of it was worthwhile and valuable. Even the heretical and marginal spiritual movements of his time – Béguines, Friends of God, Brethren of the Free Spirit – seem to have taught him something, once he had sifted out the wheat from the chaff. We can learn from this attitude of his, confronted as we are with new forms of social and communal life in South America, and ancient wisdom-traditions from the East. It is not naïve to see social and political implications in Eckhart's teaching on 'universal human nature', on spiritual detachment and poverty, on the Divine Word as supreme Justice. Neither is it naïve to see elements in his spiritual teaching which recall Hindu Vedanta and Buddhist Zen. Truth, as Eckhart saw, is one, and it is not a different truth when stated by the Bible on the one hand, and Plato or Sankara on the other. Any genuine expression of the truth in one particular place sets up resonances, or echoes, everywhere else.

As for the present book, it is now time to bring it to an end. Some may feel impelled to get to know Eckhart's own work rather better, so perhaps a few practical counsels might be in order here. He wrote in both Latin and German, and those who wish to study him in the original will need to resort to the great Kohlhammer edition mentioned in the Bibliography on page 132. Translations of the Latin works are partial and few. Their style and terminology make them difficult for the non-specialist, and their language, which sparkles in the original, emerges as curiously heavy in translation. The German works, however, are now accessible in good, English translations, the best of which is undoubtedly the recent three-volume edition by Walshe of the sermons and treatises, and the older anthology by Clark and Skinner. Details of both of these are given in the Bibliography. As a general introduction to Eckhart's thought, and exposition of its main themes, it would be hard to fault the new book by Richard Woods OP, called *Eckhart's Way*.

One who has never read Eckhart before would probably do well to start by reading a handful of sermons out of Walshe or Clark and Skinner. If the reaction is merely one of bafflement or repugnance, then it is best to go no further. If, however, interest is roused, then more sermons should be read and pondered on, and followed, perhaps, by a reading of the *Talks of Instruction*, which present the same doctrine in a less sublime and striking form, but in a homely and direct way which shows its relevance to everyday life. Finally, one can proceed to the great treatises – *On Detachment*, *The Nobleman*, *The Book of Spiritual Consolation*. These take us right into the heart of Eckhart's vision and way of life.

As for the present book, I do not wish to make any great claims for it. Its exposition of Eckhart's teaching is neither exhaustive nor particularly deep. But if it stimulates some to a deeper spiritual life and a new angle of vision, and especially if it encourages some to an exploration of Eckhart's own work, then its purpose has been amply fulfilled.

Bibliography

This is in no sense exhaustive, but merely indicates the major landmarks for anyone wishing to explore Eckhart's work in greater depth.

Eckhart's original works

Eckhart, Meister, *Die deutschen und lateinischen Werke*. Herausgegeben im Auftrage der Deutschen Forschungsgemeinschaft. 11 vols. to date. Stuttgart, Verlag W. Kohlhammer, 1936.

Translations

Clark, James M. and Skinner, John V. (eds. and trans.), *Treatises and Sermons of Meister Eckhart*. New York, Octagon Books, 1983.

Colledge, Edmund, osa and McGinn, Bernard (eds. and trans.), *Meister Eckhart: the Essential Sermons, Commentaries, Treatises and Defense*. New York, Paulist Press, and London, SPCK, 1981.

McGinn, Bernard (ed. and trans.), *Meister Eckhart: Teacher and Preacher*. New York, Paulist Press, and London, SPCK, 1986.

Walshe, M. O'C., *Meister Eckhart: Sermons and Treatises*. 3 vols. London, Element Books Ltd, 1979.

Books on Eckhart

Clark, James M., *The Great German Mystics*. New York, Russell and Russell, 1970.

Fox, Matthew, *Breakthrough: Meister Eckhart's Creation Spirituality*. New York, Doubleday, 1980.

Hustache, Jeanne Ancelet-, *Meister Eckhart*. London, Longman, 1957.

Woods, Richard, op, *Eckhart's Way*. Wilmington, Delaware, Michael Glazier, 1986; London, Darton, Longman and Todd, 1987.

Other works

Lings, Martin, *The Heralds and other poems*. 2nd rev. ed. London, Perennial Books, 1971.

Yeats, William Butler, *Selected Poetry*. Ed. A. Norman Jeffares. London, Macmillan, 1971.